Passmore

temporary

urban spaces

Florian Haydn, Robert Temel

Editors

Temporary Urban Spaces
Concepts for the Use
of City Spaces

Birkhäuser – Publishers for Architecture

Basel · Boston · Berlin

texts

projects

The quotations below are from the contributions to the conference
'tempo..rar: Temporäre Nutzungen im Stadtraum' in Vienna
in May 2003.

glossary

Affirmation

Whereas long-lasting interventions necessarily have a certain degree of affirmation, temporary projects have more latitude: the motive force is more likely to be activism than politics.

Appropriation of the city

Temporary uses are symptoms of an alternative understanding to urban planning: rather than leaving development to government and the economy alone, they explore an appropriation of the city.

Change in the culture of planning

Temporary uses also produce a change in the culture of planning.

Do-it-yourself mentality

The most important conceptual basis for starting a temporary project is a do-it-yourself mentality of the city's residents.

Dysfunctionality

But there is something else as well: 'The conception of an empty or unused space as economic fallow land is the product of a logic of exploitation that defines it as unused capital. The principle behind it, however, is based on an idea of functionality that sees only uselessness in the dysfunctionality of the unused and empty.'
Andreas Spiegl and Christian Teckert

Freeing spaces

It is not about indiscriminately weaving sites of interim use into a context but about making these gaps visible and activating them by means of freeing them.

Barbara Holub and Paul Rajakovics

Governing through the community

The economy, politics and administration can certainly put 'self-determined' trends to productive use for their own ends: '"governing through the community" is coming to play an increasingly important role. This form of power technology relies on communities assuming responsibility for themselves, and is primarily employed with the aim of executing integration programmes in so-called problem districts. [...] The ideal here is the "independent community", which is meant to cost as little as possible and simultaneously help to diminish state intervention.'

Klaus Ronneberger

Guerrilla

The interim user bears a structural similarity to the figure of the guerrilla fighter, especially in terms of his or her tactical approach. 'In this respect (leaving aside questions of hostility and war) the analogy between the guerrilla and the interim user is very appropriate: the guerrilla operates locally and is thoroughly familiar with the area in which he operates – like the interim user, who is not looking for just any old vacant building, but a particular one in a specific area with a good atmosphere. The guerrilla not only has a good knowledge of the area in which he operates, but also receives considerable support from the local population,

for whom he fights like a latter-day Robin Hood. [...] An essential point in both cases is the ideal for which they are fighting: unlike a normal soldier, the guerrilla rarely has problems with motivation.'
Peter Arlt

Institutionalising

An important aspect of temporary use is that institutionalising it usually hurts more than it helps.

Intentions

It is clear that fundamentally different intentions can be connected with temporary-use projects: 'One can work out two approaches, which, though they work with similar means, lead to results as different as could be: the first is motivated by a clearly directed economic calculation with the goal of improving a property or section of a city; the other is motivated by the knowledge of the lack of knowledge about the "correct" objectives – an effort to employ temporary uses in a process of trial and error to find new urban programmes.'
Christa Kamleithner

Interim uses

A distinction can be made between interim uses, places were there is a gap in the cycle of utilisation, which can be used in the short-term for other purposes, usually not with purely economic motives, and multiple uses, which seek to anchor other forms of use alongside the 'dominant' prescribed ones.

Interventions

Interventions are temporary intrusions in a site that seek to make alternatives evident.

Master plans

Temporary use is the opposite of the master plan: it starts out from the context and the current condition, not from a distant goal; it seeks to use what already exists rather than inventing everything anew; it is concerned with small places and brief spans of time as well as the conditions at various points in time.

Mixed uses

Testing programmes through temporary uses also has the effect that mixed uses, which are so difficult to implement in master planning but encourage urbanity, emerge of their own accord.

Multiple uses

A distinction can be made between interim uses, places were there is a gap in the cycle of utilisation, which can be used in the short-term for other purposes, usually not with purely economic motives, and multiple uses, which seek to anchor other forms of use alongside the 'dominant' prescribed ones.

Needs

Needs for temporality can result from culture (nomads), constraints (squatting, homelessness), fluctuation (age-related mobility, social climbing, growing households, displacement), lifestyle (career changers, climbers, dropouts) or in the

context of desires for security (temporary use of public space with protection from certain uses, privatisation of public space).
Jens Dangschat

Network

The metaphor of the network is central: in terms of both location and function, interim users are situated in various networks whose productive overlapping can lead to surprising possibilities.

Participation

The democratic principle of participation in urban planning risks being abused as 'governing through the community'.
Klaus Ronneberger

Play

Many interim users alluded in their projects to concepts from the Situationists, especially by employing the concept of play for processes of space and planning in the city, as well as extending material spaces into spaces for action.

Privatisation

Participation is contrasted with a trend towards privatisation.

Programmes

It would be interesting, in any case, to remain open towards the future state, so that temporary uses can serve to test and develop programmes.

Property

The principle of property in the city produces an interesting paradox: the dynamic of urban development and the needs of the city's residents are opposed to static property ownership, which represents an indolent aspect within the rapid city. Temporary users can thus make productive use of the gaps that result.

Prosumers

An essential aspect of many temporary projects is the concept of prosumers, that is, consumers who become active and themselves take over part of the production.
Hans Groiss

Public space

In the current debate over the use of public space in cities, temporary uses are seen as tools of empowerment: revealing the possibilities of space.

Roles

The most important roles in the context of a project for temporary use: interim users, 'official' users, owners, users/visitors, administration, politics, media.

Spaces for action

Many interim users alluded in their projects to concepts from the Situationists, especially by employing the concept of play for processes of space and planning in the city, as well as extending material spaces into spaces for action.

Squatting

One paradigmatic case of (more or less) temporary use is squatting: 'Compared with other large European cities, in Vienna [...] relatively few houses have been squatted. [...] Squatting and the associated demonstrations [...] in Berlin determined the housing policies [...] much more than here [in Vienna]. [...] Massive appropriations of vacant buildings left the impression that squatting was tolerated, and indeed many squats came to be legalised in rental agreements. The squatters' scene itself began to form a "squatters' council" in 1980 and ultimately managed to force out politicians who were involved in housing policy scandals. [...] The many squats in Germany face not only different policies for housing construction but also different practices of housing construction. For example, the squatters' scene grew into privately initiated [...] housing projects in which specific groups of uses live together and define for themselves the spatial and social structure of the residence.'
Sabine Pollak

Stimulation

The projects are a stimulation that questions the usual and familiar: 'Temporary spaces are models for a form of appropriation based on civic initiative; they provoke a clandestine revolt in an Austria hostile to rebellion. Realised projects contain an explosive power. They provoke the question "Why not here too?" The knowledge something can be implemented mobilises sleeping giants.'
Michael Mellauner

Strategy

Strategy is, like 'tactics', a term from a military context, where it refers to long-term war planning in contrast to short-term, more flexible battle planning. 'Strategy' means an approach that emerges from the planning desk and the sand table; it works from a position of power that is in a position to force its opponents to accept its conditions and to ignore limitations imposed by circumstances. Strategy plans for its own space, and that is a space of autonomy, where the objects, whether enemy soldiers or one's own, can be manoeuvred at will. The urban-planning equivalent of strategy is the master plan.

Tactics

Tactics is, like 'strategy', a term from a military context, where it refers to short-term battle planning in contrast to long-term, less flexible war planning. 'Tactics' means an approach from the weaker place, which is not in a position to dictate conditions to an opponent but is compelled to try to exploit relationships to its advantage, by waiting for an opportunity and exploiting it flexibly and quickly. Tacticians have to work in others' locations. The urban-planning equivalent of tactics is temporary use.

Tactical urban planning

A strategic approach to urban planning, like that seen in the twentieth century, is no longer possible today. The alternative is tactical urban planning: goals must be formulated and partners sought for their implementation who have similar, or at least compatible, goals.

Peter Arlt

Temporality

Temporality is an unusual idea for architecture and urban planning and for the uses proposed for their spaces: usually, planning is for the long term and not for rapid changes in use. Yet this very temporality offers its own qualities, which can be interesting both for planning and the economy as well as for groups of users who usually have little to do with planning or economy on the large scale. We do not apply the word 'temporality' in its literal sense to spaces and uses but rather use it to refer to such special qualities of the temporary rather than the actual duration of use.

Temporary space

All temporary uses can be called temporary space, on which the idea of the temporary is based: '[It] sees interim use [...] not so much in an experimental prototype [...] but in temporality itself, in a limited span of time, even in features of a spatial and urban quality. [...] Temporality as a prototypical phenomenon tends to counteract temporality itself. The political expression of this negative conception of temporality takes the form of excluding the very desires that are justified "merely" as a passing phenomenon.'
Andreas Spiegl and Christian Teckert

Temporary uses

Temporary uses are those that planned from the outset to be impermanent. We understand the idea of temporality to be determined not, as its literal meaning would suggest, by the duration of use: temporary uses are those that seek to derive unique qualities from the idea of temporality. That is why they differ from lasting uses, not because they have fewer resources available or because they want to prepare their location for something other that will last longer.

Introduction

Alternative planning methods are in great demand. The cause of Florian Haydn post@ florianhaydn.at this is not only an increasing dissatisfaction with traditional planning tools. Among new methods are approaches like participation, cooperation between public and private actors – the much-cited public-private partnerships – but also the use of temporary space, especially in an urban context. The latter is the subject of this Robert Temel robert.temel@ silverserver.at book. Using ten essays by experts and the documentation of a total of 35 project examples, which show different aspects of temporary uses in the city, we want to provide an overview of the current events in the cities of Europe and the United States. An expansion into other geographical areas would have to take different social and economic contexts into account and was therefore excluded. Forerunners of this publication were the European Union research project Urban Catalyst, which ran from 2001 to 2003[1] as well as the conference organized subsequently, 'tempo..rar: Temporäre Nutzungen im Stadtraum' (Temporary Uses in Urban Space) in Vienna in 2003. The basic ideas that are developed and expanded upon here originated in these contexts. Examples of the vitality of this theme are among others the Camp for Oppositional Architecture in Berlin in 2004 and the Swiss Web site *www. zwischennutzung.net*.

The spectrum of interests behind temporary uses is broad. It stretches from art projects to cultural and entertainment offerings with varying ambitions to purely commercial events. The accelera-

1 An account of this project's results will be available shortly: Philipp Oswalt, Klaus Overmeyer, Philipp Misselwitz, eds., *Urban Catalyst: Strategies for Temporary Use* (Barcelona, forthcoming).

tion of use is not least a characteristic of today's neo-liberal econo-
mies, and thus temporariness also belongs to the opponents of
those who want to use urban public space in a culturally subversive
way. With this publication we wish to show this spectrum of interests and the many-faceted nature of temporary space as well as
the variety of ways in which it is used. Temporary space is not the
recommended tool in every case, the use of which will guarantee
improvements compared with outdated methods – in each particular case the general conditions as well as interests, goals and
means must be investigated. The inclusion of process-orientated
methodology in planning, for which temporary space stands, can
bring about big advantages in comparison to a rigidly orientated
perception. In choosing projects we were influenced, on the one
hand, by an interest in clearly showing the thematic breadth of
activities and, on the other hand, by the wish to present particularly successful examples.

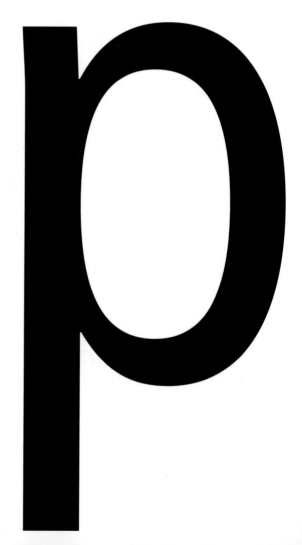

politics

ol

Temporary Uses, Deregulation and Urbanity[1]

For some time, and with increasing frequency, temporary use has turned up in the discourse on planning as a new concept, as a new urban planning method. Against the backdrop of specific examples, it seems clear what is meant. As soon as one tries to generalise from specific phenomena, however, several questions arise. What distinguishes 'temporary use' from 'normal use'? Aren't all urban uses already temporary in nature? Aren't all uses tending to become shorter in life? What is a 'use' exactly? What temporary uses achieve, it seems, is a good deal of deconstruction work: they fundamentally call planning and, even more so, its premisses, into question.

Rudolf Kohoutek, Christa Kamleithner

The Janus Face of Use

Language would have us believe that uses are the most obvious things in the world. Even Marx trusted in 'phenomenological good sense' when he spoke of a thing's *pure and simple* use value',[2] before it became exchange value and hence the fetish of commodities. 'Use' seems to be for lots, buildings and spaces what use value is for things – space as a container for sensible objectives: dwelling in a dwelling, teaching in a school building, performance

---

1 The present text was first published in *dérive: Zeitschrift für Stadtforschung,* no. 14 (2004), pp. 12–15, and is published here in a revised version.

2 Jacques Derrida, *Specters of Marx: The State of the Debt, the Work of Mourning, and the New International,* trans. Peggy Kamuf (London and New York, 1994), p. 150 (emphasis original).

in a theatre, and all that with the appropriate infrastructure and design. The concept of use thus has a Janus face: it expresses a use, a utility, and at the same time it speaks of the right of granting, as is expressed in the word 'usufruct'. A single word contains within it the transition from a practice of use, of 'function', to a legal relationship of disposition and profit, as regulated by the civil code on the basis of private property.

'Uses within the meaning of German Civil Law are the fruits and advantages of using. The term is defined in section 100 and used in various places in the German Civil Code, for example, when uses are allocated to the beneficiary or when the possessor who is not in legitimate possession vis-à-vis the owner is bound by legal action to return not only the asset itself but also its uses.'[3] 'The right to use is a permission granted by the owner of an asset or the holder of a right to use or utilise the asset or right. One specific kind of right of use is the license, which pertains to the use of a copyright, patent or other trade protection right.'[4]

Because the entire world of objects in this country is constituted as property from one end to the other, this civil right is the true constitution of uses in the city and in architecture. Use is, in any case, not a quality that is inscribed in things, buildings or spaces but rather a social relationship in the triangle of property, possession and right of use. In that sense, use is a more or less flexible relationship within which people can make various uses of one

3 www.net-lexikon.de/Nutzung.html
4 www.ratgeberrecht.de/worte/rw02130.html
5 This, in turn, is a point of departure for aesthetics, art and culture
   that makes it possible to alienate things and spaces in order to given
   them alternative meanings counter to their use value. Therein lies
   the error of a certain – mono-functional – 'functionalism' that sought
   to design the use of things and spaces in a more uniform, trouble-
   free and imperative way.

and the same thing or, expressed more generally, can relate to this thing in different ways – and thus pursue different interests.[5]

The uses regulated by building and planning codes seem so natural that architects and planners expend little thought on the specific 'constructedness' of these uses. What is, at most, discussed is the polarity of separating and mixing uses. The question of the construction of uses ultimately comes down to the question of how practical life and social processes can be parcelled and segmented in terms of space, property and time – that is to say, what of that takes place in a 'mixed' fashion, and for which separate institutions, practices and spaces have been created that are available as free supply or on the market in exchange for payment or even involve an obligation to adopt them.

It is popular to paint a relatively static picture of the 'old society' and contrast it with increasing 'deregulation': liberation from traditional ties, like those people have with concrete spaces. In fact, however, there have always been fierce battles over acquiring spaces, and they reached one climax in the nineteenth century, when the present transformations began and hence were relatively clearly separable from the previous social and spatial conditions: industrialisation and urbanisation, the constitution of a new civil society and the production of workers as autonomous individuals.

One early sign of this, for example, was the Stein-Hardenberg reforms in Germany, which fundamentally transformed spatial structure and planning codes in the early decades of the nineteenth century through several edicts that accelerated the de-territorialisation, the decoupling of buildings and residents and all sorts of other 'freedoms': freedom of domicile, that is, liberating peasants who were subjects of landlords; freedom of trade, that is, the elimination of the guilds and free disposal of land, that is, simplification of the often many-layered property and disposal rights as well as the expropriation of many peasants and the gradual elimination of communal property. This created the legal foundations to generate freely available labour forces, which were in turn the basis for the massive influx into cities and the creation of a competitive pressure previously unknown, which led to the proletarianisation of many small craftsmen and artisans.[6]

This mobilisation did not affect everyone equally; rather, it divided the population into one group that tended to be settled and another that was highly mobile, liberated by the redistribution of land, which strengthened the bourgeoisie relative to the nobility. In the cities, it resulted in a parallelism of relative fixed uses of space on the basis of long-term, stable property relations and more flexible, short-term use relations – distributed among the various social classes. For the lower classes, the changing job offerings and repeated rent increases led to frequent changes of residence at a rate scarcely imaginable today, often quarterly, so that moves were a common sight on public streets.[7] For a large portion of the urban population, 'normal' use of an apartment proved to be relatively temporary.

Temporary Uses as Society's Self-Observation

Modern architecture, which picked up on the criticism of the Wilhelmine-era city, the so-called housing question and the migra-

6 Johann Friedrich Geist and Klaus Kürvers, *Das Berliner Mietshaus,* vol. 1 (1740–1862) (Munich, 1980), pp. 72–73, 47. Wolfgang Kantzow, 'Der Bruch in der Entwicklung der deutschen Städte ausgehend von der preußischen Reformpolitik und dem veränderten Begriff des Bodeneigentums', in Gerhard Fehl and Juan Rodriguez-Lores, eds., *Stadterweiterungen, 1800–1875: Von den Anfängen des modernen Städtebaues in Deutschland* (Hamburg, 1983), pp. 25–34.

7 Clemens Wischermann, 'Mythen, Macht und Mängel: Der deutsche Wohnungsmarkt im Urbanisierungsprozess', in *Geschichte des Wohnens,* vol. 3: *Das bürgerliche Zeitalter,* 1800–1918, ed. Jürgen Reulecke (Stuttgart, 1997), p. 448.

tions it produced, led to a particularly close coupling of rooms, sections of buildings and buildings and the ways they were used (keyword: functionalism). The architectural avant-garde of the 1960s and 1970s, in turn, showed a pronounced interest in the themes of flexibility and variability, long before the emergence of the new information, communication and work technologies, the new just-in-time forms, increased flexibility and deregulation of markets and institutions (which, despite appearances, is concerned only with a more stable acquisition of property in more private and more profitable forms) set such tasks for architects.

That urban life – urbanity, as we are in the habit of saying, as image and as process – cannot be optimally processed within the spatial separations of functionalism, is one issue. Another is that it is only partially compatible with stable private ownership of land. Yet another, related aspect is that there are numerous activities within the whole spectrum of urban uses, for which the private real estate market has only inadequate supply. If this was true of the last century and the one before it, it remains true for the present, in altered form, now against the backdrop of a further acceleration of the cycles of utilisation and a general mobilisation. Whereas the Austrian zoning categories correspond to the conventional markets for residences, offices and industrial areas on the basis of private ownership of property and buildings and long-term occupation, increasingly a contradiction is becoming evident between the normal economy of private utilisation of space and the demands of an 'urban economy'.[8]

8 See also the final report of the Magistratsabeilung 18 – Stadtentwicklung und Stadtplanung of the City of Vienna on the EU research
   project 'Urban Catalyst: Strategien für temporäre Nutzungen; Entwicklungspotentiale für urbane Residualflächen in europäischen Metropolen',
   published in *Werkstattberichte,* no. 60, ed. Stadtplanung Wien,
   Magistratsabteilung 18, Vienna, 2003, esp. pp. 56ff.

The concept of 'urban economy' is supposed to be understood to mean the totality of all activities and uses that are important for a city. They can, however, also be viewed as barter systems, though some of them fall out of the framework of profitable exchange, as only very low rents can be afforded. Many of the groups responsible for such demand are, moreover, unstable and too far from established markets to be able to accumulate enough capital to compete with the demand in urban real estate markets or even to purchase space. These include a range of social uses, such as club activities, space for children and young people etc., in general social activities that need space but not over the long term; or in the field of culture, which has long since grown out of the classical sites for culture and places for popular culture and needs flexible spaces of all sizes. Another variety of the urban economy is encouraging innovation: start-ups and the network of so-called creative industries, which need special spaces and production conditions that the normal market offers only on an inadequate scale or at unaffordable prices.

In these fields it is evident that within the framework of the usual legal relationships and planning procedures, it is difficult to activate a whole series of central urban uses; they evidently fall outside of the 'normal economy'. In order to create room for such activities anyway, more and more frequently, particularly in the context of art and culture, legally precarious situations are being tolerated that on the basis of their contracts alone represent only 'temporary use'.[9] To the extent that they represent an economic and legal exception, temporary uses are uses for which a society does not usually provide space, and they use spaces that, for whatever rea-

9 One such insecure legal form, which means only minimal costs for uses (limited to overhead, insurance, etc.) is the so-called *Prekarium* under section 974 of the Austrian Civil Code, a contract that can be terminated by either party at any time.

son, stand vacant, and hence lie in the shadows of social or private attention. Temporary users observe social relations and exploit gaps and niches. The paradoxical aspect of this is that, on the one hand, vacancies are continually being recorded – and are increasing – and, on the other, the cities urgently need any kind of revitalisation and innovation in their policies regarding locational competition. It remains to be seen whether temporary uses present a solution to this problem or could lead to a new way of thinking about urban planning.

Similar questions are already being asked from the official perspective and in relation to 'normal', large-scale urban uses. For example, the Deutsches Institut für Urbanistik (Difu), at the behest of the Ministry of Labour, Social and Urban Development, Culture and Sports of the Land of North Rhine-Westphalia, has produced a 'study of the specific economic utilisation times of urban planning functions and facility types', which raises the fundamental question of the 'time intervals of utilisation cycles in commercial real estate and lots'. It addresses the 'accelerated tempo of converting real estate in various branches' with the risk of vacancy, unutilised properties and specific risks from such runaway investment that is largely irresponsible vis-à-vis the city.[10]

From the perspectives of city planning and social critique, this deregulation is lamentable; as this Difu study suggests, it is possible to develop several additional instruments of control, either restrictions or financial measures, and otherwise just watch as the

10 www.difu.de/forschung: 'Retail properties in smaller centres and highly specialised real estate in the leisure industry are at greater risk of disuse as time passes.' 'As a precaution against long-term vacancy, it has been proposed to require compulsory insurance to finance deconstruction and returning the site to a natural state.' It is interesting that the possibility of 'returning the site to a natural state' is considered but not making it available for uses that require low-cost space.

'old urbanity' in cities increasingly wastes away while debating which social, economic and cultural values the 'new urbanity' should have: urban events culture, street markets, cafés, pedestrian zones and shopping malls. Another inference from this would be countering the passively endured deregulation with another, positive, programmatic deregulation of uses in relation to long-term property and 'normal utilisation' in the form of temporary uses.

This would mean that cities need a supplementary praxis for using space that adroitly – through minimal extensions of planning and building codes – operates with vacant spaces, niches and time windows in the course of changes in use as a way of balancing out urban disparities. Temporary uses would thus align with a movement – whose effects are diverse, and sometimes ambivalent – that is occurring anyway as part of deregulation and increasing flexibility of the use of space, namely, sequential use of public spaces for events; management of park space on the basis of different times and circles of authorised uses; new time limits in rental law; vast deregulation of career paths and its effects on living situations, etc.[11] Temporary uses could, perhaps, interpret the paradigm of deregulation in new and different ways.

11 All these 'movements' doubtless operate within the field of a violent tension between processes of massive deregulation and new determinations, concentrations of capital that actively and passively free up a rich variety of nomadic currents indirectly through the impact of imminent unemployment, the destruction of the know-how of small companies, the radical concentration of book, newspaper and other media markets, etc.

Temporary Uses as Programme

In the United States, for example, the phrase 'temporary use' is found in many planning and building ordinances; it is the collective term for uses of brief duration that are, to a greater or lesser extent, listed on assessment roles, ranging from Christmas tree markets, model homes and construction or sales offices of developers. This American pragmatism surely explains why an Internet search (on Google) using the English phrase 'temporary uses' produces more than 60,000 hits, but just 500 for the German phrase 'temporäre Nutzungen', more than half of which stem from the circle of the European Union project Urban Catalyst.[12] Here 'temporary uses' do not simply follow pragmatic demands but represent rather a programmatic concept that derives from certain historic 'uses', or rather events, in the circles of the sub-, counter- and alternative culture[13] a methodology or strategy for urban planning.

The appropriation of a rundown loft as a sculpture studio or the 'squatting' of an old, disused abattoir and its transformation into an 'arena' for alternative culture – the most spectacular example of squatting in Vienna, back in 1976 – is a long way to a new programme for temporary uses and their solid protection under the civil code and planning and building codes. Art obtained, retained or conquered a certain degree of freedom when the modern systems of function were elaborated, which in the meanwhile has

12 See note 8 and www.urbancatalyst.net.
13 Temporary uses include appropriations of lots and buildings for the use of the subculture, by methods that range from the more or less peaceful to the subversive – i.e., 'squatting'; forms of temporary appropriation of private land, as has been (and is) tolerated in various countries when there are both vacant buildings and emergency needs (Italy, Great Britain, the Netherlands, or in the *favelas* of South America).

been handed over by the system. Hence art is permitted to 'play' – but only in a symbolic way – even with private property and many other social institutions, exploring their boundaries and thematising differences. Although the Arena was cleared by force by the police after a 'season' of a hundred days in 1976, in the meanwhile cultural temporary uses have become an official – if still contested – programme in urban development projects, such as the site of a former cable-making factory in the Meidling district of Vienna. Temporary uses are already part of the fixed repertoire of the events culture of European cities.

Temporary uses in the social field would mean something completely different, for this field is encoded quite differently than that of art and culture. The social realm lies in the responsibility of the state and of the 'well off', which is why appropriation of private property by the homeless or unemployed would provoke the system more than it comes from the art world. A minimal social benefit is provided by the state; the rest is supposed to be covered by private, voluntary charity or behind church doors.[14] Temporary uses from 1968 to the present were in that respect essentially sub-cultural, limited-term appropriation of space for explicitly articulated 'personal need in an extended sense'. Thus there was, and still is, a remnant of a bohemian bonus being consumed. The dominant order can endure selective self-questioning only in artistic and culture matters, not in moral and political ones. Going beyond

---

14 Exceptions include temporary uses that have already been officialy recognised and that are related both to the general deregulation and dwindling financial resources of public bodies and to the recognition of the positive qualities of the temporary and ephemeral include, for example, schoolrooms (e.g., schools on a ship, rented classrooms, lectures in vacant cinemas, all of which have been done in Vienna), temporary uses for children and young people (e.g., einfach-mehrfach, the Viennese magistrate's coordination centre for multiple use) and so on.

that, recognizing the demand for space from many urban and social uses with little opportunity on the free market and then translating it into property and planning law would be a genuinely interesting aspect of a practice of temporary use.

It is a practice, however, that will remain ambivalent: before limited-term uses can be elevated to a programme, we should recall that, to an unbelievable extent, 'temporary uses' are most directly connected with wars, expulsions and natural catastrophes. For the most part, temporary uses result from shortages. It is far from obvious how this can be turned into something positive, but such an effort corresponds to today's positive assessment of the nineteenth-century metropolis and its 'urbanity', which is tied to temporalising use. Whereas modern urban planning was founded in opposition to this form of the city and hence overlooked its positive facets, today there is a tendency to overlook the poverty and misery that living and work situations entailed for most immigrants (and still do).

The nineteenth-century city was shaped by the logic of a real estate market that was based on utilisation cycles, not idealised final states. The flexibility of buildings from the Wilhelmine era, which is seen so positively today, was a reaction to the new situation of building for a need that was only partly known and was also the result of a search for the maximum possible, enduring utility and profitability. That is why the transformation of various flat sizes and of residential and commercial space was certainly planned and why conversions within certain general parameters were part of its programme.[15] The users with little financial means might often have had to put up with disagreeable situations, like apartments divided by a common hallway or near the noise and stench

15 See Johann Friedrich Geist and Klaus Kürvers, *Das Berliner Mietshaus,* vol. 2 (1862–1945) (Munich, 1984), pp. 222, 266ff., 284ff.

of small business. Such circumstances are most evident in older sections of the city, in which the old building fabric was refurbished.

It is not obvious how one is to derive a positive conception of urbanity from this: the multiple use or repurposing of space, overlapping uses and the resulting 'density' are all the result of a shortage, whereas the isolation and dispersion of individual uses and their 'appropriate' rehousing in specific buildings, in keeping with the logic of functionalism, were initially an indication of increasing wealth. In the meanwhile, however, it has become clear that it went hand in hand with an experience of loss: the gap between intended and practiced use and the refurbishing of the old building fabric involved wealth as well. The recombination of buildings and uses produced situations that, to borrow from Robert Venturi, are marked by 'complexity and contradiction'; they question desires for particular uses and compel adaptations, but they also permit new interpretations and unforeseen constellations.[16]

This, however, no longer happens automatically when high vacancy rates or constantly new construction becomes manageable as a result of new investment strategies and technologies of production, which causes the real estate market to function very differently. The increasing temporalisation of uses can relate to the building stock in diverse ways: it can lead to urban planning as urban recycling; at the moment it tends to lead to buildings with ever-shorter lives, which are intended to quickly fulfil a market and

---

16 See Walter Siebel, 'Einleitung', in idem, ed., *Die europäische Stadt* (Frankfurt am Main, 2004), p. 50: 'Urbanity has within it a tense relationship, between physical proximity and social distance, between density and aloofness, between historical meaning and current use. Such productive tension concentrates in particular places at particular times, there were a new society is appropriating the shells of a society that has become historic.'

make a profit and then be abandoned as soon as circumstances change. If the former introduces a historical dimension to 'use' – forcing one to come to terms with older uses that are embodied in existing architectural forms – the latter amounts to an accelerated functionalism that lines up seemingly ideal situations, one after the other, without being able to network them. This also has ecological consequences that can scarcely be estimated yet, and it leads to a social and functional disentanglement that thus far has produced few convincing new urban spaces.

The fact that temporary uses now have to be seen from the planners' perspective as sensible and programmatic aspects of a process-based approach to planning is closely related to these developments. This kind of postmodern understanding of planning is a not insignificant novelty in the history of urban planning: any form of planning would start out from the limited nature of uses and the convertibility of buildings, from the various possibilities for translating needs for use into building structures and relating the two. It would thus significantly change the conception of planning.

This rethinking is certainly connected with the failure of modern planning, but it is also an effect of two centuries of the disintegration of traditional architectural forms and the dissolution of the bond between buildings, residents and 'uses', in part through the real estate market, which thereby performed, quite accidentally, a task of 'architectural criticism'.

Urban Planning and Interim Use[1]

Interim use and long-term use

Interim users exploit interruptions in use that occur when a build- Peter Arlt
ing has been standing empty for a while or when spaces are left
unused. This is the case, for instance, when an investor is unable
to execute a plan for a specific use because planning schedules,
legal disputes and so on make it impossible to use a property for
a while. Interim users exploit these transitional periods and use
spaces, rooms and buildings for other purposes. Interim use is always seen as a provisional measure rather than as a permanent
solution, although it can also be a way of demonstrating a concept's success in order to convince an investor that the chosen use
could also provide a permanent solution. This line of approach is
rarely adopted, however. Normally, specific measures have to be
implemented at a certain location within set deadlines. However,
many (but not all) interim users are not looking for a long-term or
permanent solution, but want to carry out projects in full awareness that they will be of short duration.

In principle, there is nothing 'alternative' about interim use: every
supermarket, for example, erects its new hall at a profitable location and tears it down again once it has paid itself off and ceases
to operate as successfully as desired. Enterprises are set up at certain locations because they receive grants to create jobs there;
they leave these locations as soon as they have fulfilled the con-
tractual obligations tied to those grants. Interim use is one of the
fundamental classical principles of the market economy. Utilisation
cycles are becoming shorter and shorter, and capital is proving to
be extremely flexible when it comes to changing locations. Tem-

---

1 The following text is based on an interview with Peter Arlt.

porariness is thus a principle of our present time and not a specific phenomenon related to interim use alone. In this respect, interim use suits the system.

Places

Interim users select sites that are of no interest to real-estate investors at a certain time. During the 1990s, the advanced state of decline of a great many of the so-called *Gründerzeit* buildings (dating from the late 19th century) in the eastern part of Berlin acted as a break on potential large-scale investment. As years passed, however, interim users turned their attention to other parts of the city. By the year 2000, *Gründerzeit* buildings had already started losing their appeal for them because these buildings had become fashionable places to live in. (This was the case in Berlin-Mitte and Prenzlauer Berg, for example.) The principle of living in a *Gründerzeit* building, which had become widely accepted in the West in the 1980s, had now caught on in the East, too, causing many West Berliners and West Germans to move there. As space became increasingly scarce, investors sensed its potential, and pressure to use it increased dramatically. Consequently, people began to turn their attention to buildings constructed in the 1950s and 1960s. The new locations are always those that fail to become the target of 'official' interest during a certain period. In the meantime, there is widespread interest in buildings dating from the 1950s and 1960s, too. One can therefore assume that interim users have already begun searching for the next new locations. It is always a case of making new discoveries and re-evaluating them. Quite likely, the vacant bankrupt Cineplex Centres will be the next target of interest.

Has interim use now acquired the same importance it had in Berlin in the 1990s? At the time, the vast number of empty buildings and the lack of pressure to exploit them created a special situation in Berlin. Such situations offer interim users a large choice of interesting sites; indeed, if such a choice didn't exist, there would be no interim users. At about the same time, there was far greater pressure to exploit properties in Vienna than in Berlin, with the result that there were incomparably fewer vacant buildings there. Consequently, the interim-users' scene in Vienna could have nowhere near same kind of cultural impact on Vienna as a whole as its counterpart in Berlin. Hence, interim use remained a comparatively marginal phenomenon in Vienna's cultural scene.

Actors

Unification created a very special situation in Berlin. The city became a Mecca for everyone involved in art and culture, attracting many involved in these areas as well as others who had contacts in the scene. Together, they formed a huge 'critical mass' with the potential to evolve from a rather marginal scene into a vital cultural factor affecting the city as a whole.

Unlike the squatters' scene, from which they emerged, interim users tend to be business people, as many of Berlin's clubs show.

The media became interested in this scene because of the great contribution it made to Berlin's image. Often mentioned in the media, this scene now appears in every Berlin guide. On the other hand, in the very club scene that frequently owed its development to interim users, people are beginning to abandon the interim-use principle. With many of the clubs moving premises several times and their operators growing older, the latter now show an increasing preference for permanent locations.

Cultural interim use, as described here, is not a private form of use that turns away from the public, as was the case with the squatters, for example, but one that addresses the public. Interim users seldom had the political ambitions of the squatters, who wanted to create their own alternative world. Areas like the Berlin-Mitte

and the Prenzlauer Berg of the 1990s now accommodate a very homogenous public, including many who went to Berlin to study and then chose to stay there. They see the scene as an integral part of the city. In the meantime, however, some of them are leaving Berlin-Mitte because they find the structure too homogenous. They want to live in areas with a greater social mix. The older residential areas had already gone up market to such an extent that they began to attract investors, going through the classical phases in a gentrification process that would have happened in Berlin-Mitte in any case, but which was now being accelerated by the local cultural scene.

Strategy and Tactics

In analyses of spatial processes, the terms strategy and tactics frequently appear without any attempt being made to distinguish clearly between them. The classical definition is to be found in Clausewitz' book *Vom Kriege*[2]. Whereas the strategist has the power and money to achieve his goals without having to show too much concern for external conditions, the tactician must pay great attention to both circumstances and his adversaries. Interim users, however, are less concerned with coming to terms with adversaries, but in dealing with other actors, the property situation, media interests and visitors. The tactician also wants to achieve a specific goal, but to do so, he must be able to skilfully rope in others. He must know exactly how others are going to react and also make a far greater effort to achieve his goal by working with – rather than in opposition to – others. This does not yet make this a common goal, however. A tactician must be able to transform forces alien to himself into forces that take him to his

2 Carl von Clausewitz, *Vom Kriege* (On War) (Reinbek, 1978), p. 98, p. 179ff.

goal. It is of no consequence to him whether others reach their goals at the same time: it does not disturb him in principle. This approach is typical of the interim user, because he has the political influence neither to do what he wants with a place of his choice nor to buy a building. He has to co-operate with alien powers, win them over to his cause and get them working for him.

Guerrillas

A further analogy can be made between the interim user and the guerrilla: the guerrilla is never a strategist, he is the classic tactician. He draws his strength from his surroundings because he does not take the side of state power, he fights it. In this respect (leaving aside questions of hostility and war) the analogy between the guerrilla and the interim user is very appropriate: the guerrilla operates locally and is thoroughly familiar with the area in which he operates – like the interim user, who is not looking for just any old vacant building, but a particular one in a specific area with a good atmosphere. The guerrilla not only has a good knowledge of the area in which he operates, but also receives considerable support from the local population, for whom he fights like a latter-day Robin Hood. Interim users are also popular – not only with local residents, but with the media too. An essential point in both cases is the ideal for which they are fighting: unlike a normal soldier, the guerrilla rarely has problems with motivation. The interim user also fights for his own cause and is highly motivated, regardless of whether a building is to be used as a club, a gallery or a bar. Furthermore, the interim user is never interested in money alone, but in putting his ideas into practice. Consequently, an interim user is interested in a smooth transition between work and leisure, between independent activity and private life. In this respect, the interim user is a pioneer of capitalist economics, which demands that its workers show a high degree of personal identification with their work, their workplace and the company, and overcome the strict separation between work and leisure time. The only difference is that the interim user is working on his own project and not for someone else.

Tactical urban planning

This distinction is also applicable to the field of urban planning: for, in theory, an authority entrusted with urban planning still has the political power to operate like a strategist, but it no longer has the resources. The authority depends on private support, and the type of co-operation required here is based on the public-private partnership (PPP) established between private and public actors to implement, for example, urban-planning projects. Meanwhile, urban authorities seem to be responding in an increasingly defensive manner, leaving decisions increasingly to the private sector (i.e. to investors), and forgetting that a tactician also has his own goals, which he wishes to achieve – albeit in a tactical manner – on the basis of co-operation. Such goals can, of course change in the course of the planning process: if, for instance, observations and experiments suggest that a different approach might be more suitable than the original one. However, this does not alter the basic goal in any way.

As far as the question of interim use is concerned, the important point is that these PPPs rely on big investors for implementation and that they function. This is not the case with small interim users, however. For even though they could make a great contribution to the goals of a urban-planning department, they are generally rejected as partners. And even where contacts are established, communication between the parties involved tends to be difficult. Urban planners ought to learn to operate with and make use of these small initiatives as well; for, after all, they too are investors. Hence, PPPs should be extended to include the smaller groupings and the cultural scene. Instead of operating only strategically on the basis of property alignments and assigned uses, an effort should be made to find out what kind of district or city would make sense, to see what initiatives exist that might promote developments to achieve this goal, and to establish how they can be supported. Here, urban planning could endeavour to harmonise the interests of large and small investors. Small investors can only provide small sums of money; in some cases, all they have to offer is their labour time. However, they do have strengths that large developers lack, for instance: activities, life, and regularity. Interim users bring buildings and streets to life, and thus have a positive impact on the district as a whole. Enthusiasm is the capital of interim users, and urban planners should recognise this and use it tactically. Sometimes, it is easier to forge coalitions between large and small investors than between the authorities and interim users. However, the authorities have also become aware of this problem, as the *Raumpioniere in Berlin*[3] (Space Pioneers in Berlin), an exhibition financed by the City of Berlin, demonstrates. In Berlin, models financed by the city now exist that support interim uses not only in the centre, but also on the outskirts, as in the district of Marzahn-Hellersdorf,[4] for example. There is also a private agency for interim uses.[5] In Vienna, the urban co-ordination office einfach-mehrfach for interim and multiple uses has been running for several years now. For many years, the Berlin authorities had little time for interim-use projects. A large part of the scene in the district of Berlin-Mitte only came into being because it was

3 A study, symposium and exhibition on temporary uses in Berlin 2004–2005 undertaken by the studio Urban Catalyst and commissioned by the Berlin Senate Department for Urban Development.
4 The initiative Tausche Fläche gegen Nutzungsidee (Exchange Space for an Idea on how to Use It) launched by Plattform Marzahn-Hellersdorf.
5 www.zwischennutzungsagentur.de (26 January 2006)

supported by one employee, Jutta Weitz, who worked for the public urban development corporation the Wohnungsbaugesellschaft Mitte (WBM). (Jutta Weitz was responsible for buildings whose ownership status awaited clarification.) In many cases, she handed properties over to interim users for cultural projects, demanding little more than the operating costs in return.

This kind of approach, which seeks partnerships and allies in order to achieve its goals, was supposed to become the new model for municipal planners. If one no longer has the opportunity to make a decision sitting at one's desk, then one has to start communicating with lots of different people and concerns. One needs to walk through the city with one's eyes open and observe developments in order to find out who might be responsive to the goals one has set oneself as a urban planner and to offer these people support. The tactician is always on the move, whereas the strategist sits at his desk, observing through the window perhaps – and from a distance – the places where he works. The urban planner has to be right there where the action is.

From Regulation to Moderation

When discussing temporary spaces, people often proceed from Klaus Ronneberger the hypothesis that our model for urban development is no longer the master plan conceived on the drawing board, but temporary uses that are already available at a specific place and programmes that have evolved within a specific context – 'organically' as it were – with the participation of the local population. Indeed, there seems to be no question of a return to a grand plan, at least as far as the political institutions and the urban-planning disciplines are concerned. There are a number of reasons for this change in strategy. Before I begin to examine these more closely, I should first like to historically situate the term 'temporary use'.

Temporary Use and the Situationists

The terminology has its roots in the theoretical models dating from the late 1950s. At the time, the Situationist International (SI), responding to the homogenising and disciplining effects of functional urban planning, formulated a new approach to the social space of the city. The proposals of the Situationists for the 'rational beautification' of the City of Paris were programmatic in nature. They called for the Metro stations to be opened every night, for roofs to be designed so that people could take walks on them, for churches to be converted into children's playgrounds, for the abolition of museums and the distribution of the art works among pubs and cafés. At the same time, the Parisian market halls were to be relocated to the outskirts and the buildings replaced by a series of small complexes, which would serve as 'a pleasure ground where workers can learn through play'. What the Situationists were in fact demanding were mobile urban spaces and a modifiable architecture that could be partially or totally transformed in tune with their inhabitants' desires. In addition to the idea of using cultural products for purposes other than those originally intended, they also proposed 'roaming' as another key area for subversive practice. The aim of these 'psycho-geographical' explorations was to bring out the social aspects of the topography and the affective dimensions of constructed space. The urban implementation of the Situationist programme, which included banishing all things functional and exploring the variability of space for playful activities, culminated in the concept of a city subject to a continuous, active process of construction and decay. The new construction technologies seemed to transcend the opposition between the permanent and the temporary and thus make it possible to combine structuring activities and mobility. Soon, however, the more radical elements among the Situationists abandoned these architectural models in favour of a more subversive critique of contemporary urbanism. They denounced the notion that novel spaces would almost inevitably lead to new social relations as bourgeois ideology.

Even though the avant-garde ideas of the Situationists had a manifestly playful character, they were nonetheless based on the fundamental premise that it was necessary to relate the constructed environment to the social context and to conceive space as a product of social activity. This perspective was systematised by the French philosopher Henri Lefebvre, who was in close contact with the Situationists for a time: urban space was seen as both a product and a medium; created by social praxis, it also structured society. Henri Lefebvre developed a complex schema for precisely defining socio-spatial processes. The first dimension represents *perceived* space, and is concerned with the collective production of urban reality, in other words: with the rhythms of work, home life and leisure activities in which a society decodes and reproduces its spatiality. Then next dimension is that of *imagined* space, shaped by forms of knowledge, as well as by signs and codes. This level involves 'representations of space', in other words: the constructions of urban planners, architects and other specialists who break space down into individual elements and then 'reassemble' it a-new. This level is dominant in capitalist society, where prevailing discourse is attuned to exploitation, quantification and administration in line with market requirements, thus legitimating and supporting various functional modes of capital and the state. Finally, there is *experienced* and *suffered* space. This level deals with 'spaces of representation', that is: space as it is experienced by users of both sexes and mediated through the images and symbols of everyday life. This space contains the possibility of resistance.

Ideologies of Space

This schema is useful in understanding the transformation of urban discourse and practices. Hence, the conceptive ideologies of the modernists were based on the idea of treating the industrial city as both a mechanical unit and a huge integrative machine. During the twentieth century, this model evolved into what one might refer to as the Fordist city, as an important dispositive of the welfare state. Fordism was all about quantitatively increasing the volume of production and spatially extending industrial structures. Viewing a national territory as a whole and as the decisive geographical unit, it contended that a framework of 'central places' would ensure steady growth and overcome existing socio-spatial disparities. The goal was to 'homogenise living conditions' and create fair welfare conditions for society as a whole. This interventionist model, which was based on the central state, tried to restrict local independent initiative, which it perceived as 'narrow-minded particularism'. Communities were assigned the role of mere 'transmission belts', whose main function was to implement administratively instructions issued 'from above'. Functionalism became the dominant ideology of space: it not only established, for several decades, a certain degree of cohesion between urban planning, politics and everyday activities, but also co-ordinated diverse social practices. The urban development disciplines sought to create a homogeneous space united through all the separations between work, home and transportation. An urbanisation model thus came into being that strove to standardise the everyday lives of city inhabitants by organising space on the basis of a serial grid. In a certain way, then, one could grasp the urban power matrix of Fordism as a variant of Foucault's disciplining society. During the 1970s, social movements arose in very different constellations that were opposed to both a rationalised everyday life and functionalist modernisation strategies. The growing criticism of de-urbanisation was subsequently taken up by the urban disciplines under catchwords and phrases such as 'reprivatising the cities' and 'urbanity'.

This was also the decade in which the political economy of the Fordist growth model experienced a twofold crisis. On the one hand, the productivity reserves of the Taylorist division of labour were being depleted whilst, on the other hand, the Keynesian welfare state instruments were beginning to fail as the economy became increasingly internationalised. Furthermore, as the gap between the truly societal conflict potential and the state's ability to solve problems widened, criticism of the regulatory practice of Fordist institutions grew. Up to a point, Neoliberalism has taken up this critique of the welfare state and used it against the subjects: the new power technologies associated with Neoliberalism are designed to individualise social risks, do away with traditional protective rights and make people responsible for regulating their own lives. The new regime responds to growing demands for individual creative space by 'offering' individuals an opportunity to participate actively in solving problems hitherto regulated by state institutions.

The urban system is also undergoing a fundamental transformation. To overstate the case, one might say that whereas the metropolises used to be defined by their relationship to the processing of material resources, they now function as centres of production and of the transfer of symbols and knowledge. The declining industrial base and the growing importance of the tertiary sector have triggered a process of social polarisation. The social space of the city has become both more hierarchical and fragmentary at the same time. At that moment when the central state proved neither able nor willing to adequately balance out growing disparities in social spaces by providing funds and other forms of assistance, local development models became increasingly important. In contrast to the 1970s, where the aim was to overcome inequalities in spaces by establishing uniformity at the national level, the state now tends to gamble on the local level. Cities feel obliged to develop corporate profiles and play an active role in local labour and social policy. The central issue for local state policy is no longer to provide social infrastructures, as was the case in the past, but to organise urban space in line with the needs of the market. The decisive features of the 'entrepreneurial city' are its abandonment of the statist solidarity principle and the mobilisation of space as a strategic resource.

New Territorial Strategies

Urban development policy's new focus has also inspired a succession of new territorial strategies. Hence, urban management is now hastening the development of the core city into a kind of consumer-cum-events landscape for wealthier sections of the population and affluent tourists. To this end, the model of the European city is also being revived against historical backdrops. Not only that, highly concentrated spatial units are also being created around city centres, uniting in various ways the workplace, the home, shopping and entertainment facilities. Municipal planning policy is also devoting attention to these two dominant forms of urban planning. Frequently, key urban-planning projects are now being implemented by public-private partnerships funded by the authorities and private investors. At the same time, local authorities are gradually surrendering their responsibility for the city as a whole, concentrating their activities and resources on specific areas instead, and hoping to notch up exemplary successes, albeit at the expense of a more broadly conceived intervention policy. Entrepreneurial strategy follows the logic of growing economic competition between urban centres, hierarchising urban space by focusing on isolated fragments and, at the same time, exploding the framework of modern urban planning by executing huge projects. At the present level of globalisation and flexibalisation of the economy, Fordism's territorial organisation is becoming an obstacle to more mobile flows of capital and information. A new network of privileged intersections is imposing itself on Fordist spatial structures and tearing apart the extensive functional grids.

Two more territorial strategies are emerging alongside the 'politics of privileged space'. On the one hand, municipalities are attempting not only to tighten their control over fragmented urban space with a variety of regulatory strategies, but also to squeeze any submilieus that adversely affect consumption out of centrally located squares and open areas. On the other hand, 'governing through the community' is coming to play an increasingly important role. This form of power technology relies on communities assuming responsibility for themselves and is primarily employed with the aim of executing integration programmes in so-called problem districts. Local residents are being empowered and included in decision-making processes that affect their own lives, the goal being to encourage people affected by decisions to act for themselves. This may seem surprising at first sight, but those affected are subordinate groups of people who, in the past, have tended to be strictly regimented by state organisations and charities. However, in this social area, too, there is a noticeable increase in the use of intervention techniques that are designed to empower people, to encourage them to act on their own responsibility by taking charge of their own lives and to share the responsibility for creating a successful community.

In the Federal Republic of Germany, this mobilisation programme goes under the name of 'the activating state'. The advocates of this concept explicitly distance themselves from the model of the 'slender state', which they see as failing to move beyond merely cutting public expenditure. The 'activating state', in contrast to the interventionist welfare state, is not supposed to control society directly, but only support it by moderating its 'self-development'. In Germany, for instance, this model has assumed the form of the nation-wide *social city* programme pursued by various initiatives in the federal states. Ever since the central state compelled the cities to adopt municipal self-help programmes in the eighties, the cities have been shifting the responsibility for economic and social development to the various districts. These programmes place particular emphasis on mobilising local resources, developing self-supporting structures and encouraging residents to help themselves. In a certain way then, municipal modernisation policies thus instrumentalise local actors and forms of self-organisation in order to curb counter-trends that result in the abolition of social programmes and, consequently, in impoverishment too. For quite some time now, social initiatives challenging urban rehabilitation programmes controlled by the central state have been demanding that planning guidelines be anchored in the local population. In the meantime, however, the political scenario has changed completely. In the 1970s, participation models were still largely confined to getting citizens to participate in planning projects. Later on, local authorities co-operated with countless local projects (most of which had arisen in protest against municipal rehabilitation programmes) in 'social municipal rehabilitation schemes'. Nowadays, 'self-participation' and 'residents' participation' are invoked quite frequently and unashamedly in so-called problem districts. The ideal here is the 'independent community', which is meant to cost as little as possible and simultaneously help to diminish state intervention.

As social and power structures have changed, the once predominant master plan has been largely discredited as a model. Although the traditional planning instruments still exist, the central and local authorities no longer have the resources or political will to apply them. Nowadays, it is not the establishment of spatial structures based on planning concepts of scale, but the organisation and moderation of processes that are creating the conditions for further urban development. At the same time, a pragmatic approach has gained currency that degrades the planning authorities to the status of executive organs serving the particular interests best able to assert themselves.

Development strategies that reflect these types of power constellations must therefore take into consideration the greater whole and avoid defining any one spatial level as *the* decisive field of action. It would be far better to link urban-planning schemes at a number of different levels with projects that focus on social space: i.e. horizontally between the community and the region, and vertically between the local, national and even transnational levels. As urban centres cannot be confined within local boundaries, and power relations are produced and reproduced in diverse spatial units, a perspective is needed that seeks to transcend the individual territorial levels and hence the boundaries of the district and the city too. A policy of jumping scales could open the door to new forms of urban practice that are opposed to neo-liberal territorial strategies.

The Temporary in the City

Cities have long lives, and urban planning has long-term effects, Robert Temel
so how is the temporary relevant to the city? 'Temporary' refers to
something that exists for a time, but there are different concepts
of such temporariness: 'Ephemeral' is a term from biology that
refers to creatures that live for only a day. Ephemerality is thus an
existential temporality; the ephemeral has a short life, its existence
cannot be extended. This contrasts with the provisional, which begins as something with a short life but then, not infrequently, remains for very long periods. 'Provisional' refers to a facility that is
conceived as a mere substitute for the 'real thing', the lasting, an
interim measure when something is needed but the quality one
would truly like cannot yet be achieved, but will perhaps be possible at a later point. The temporary stands between these two
positions. It is, on the one hand, short-lived like the ephemeral,
but unlike the latter it can certainly exist for a longer period than
was initially intended. It is possible to extend its life. In that respect
it shares qualities with the provisional, but the temporary also has
its own qualities and should not be viewed as merely a substitute
for the fully adequate. This special quality can, for example, be
that temporal limitation permits many things that would still be
inconceivable if considered for the long term. Things that would
be unbearable over the long term can still be perceived as valuable
for the short term. The adjective 'temporary' is often linked to concepts that in fact stand for long-lived things – for example, temporary buildings that are intended, exceptionally, to exist only for a
short time. When the concept of temporality is applied according-
ly to the practice of urban use and urban planning, it is clear that
the city as a whole will still have a long life, as it always has, but

that the practice of urban use and urban planning will lend it certain qualities that the temporary, as opposed to the long-lived, has to offer, for whatever reason.

Temporary Urbanism

One reason for appreciating these qualities lies in the requirements of an accelerated capitalist economy, which conflict with the immobility of real estate. As stated in the *Communist Manifesto:* 'All fixed, fast frozen relations, with their train of ancient and venerable prejudices and opinions, are swept away, all new-formed ones become antiquated before they can ossify.' Hence when one speaks of temporary use it is also a matter of liberating land as a means of production from the fetters of the permanent, whether in the form of, on the one hand, interim uses that make it possible to utilise unproductive idle times or, on the other, of making every use temporary on principle, since the market requires that every use give way to the next, more productive one. Hence temporality is no longer a specific quality but rather becomes something universally applicable.

But the economy is not all that matters. Temporality also relates directly to more recent approaches to urban planning, of which Margaret Crawford's 'everyday urbanism' is one example. It is concerned with small, temporary, unintentional, inexpressive but nonetheless highly frequented locations as opposed to standardised, expensive, permanent and large-scale urban planning projects, which not infrequently end up as ghost towns. 'Everyday urbanism' looks to the quotidian, to spaces between residential space, work space and institutions. In contrast to large-scale planning, 'everyday urbanism' is specific rather than normative, reacting to existing situations and attempting to reinforce their qualities. Heterogeneity is not an adversary but rather a goal. Temporary urbanism is part of this concept. In Crawford's work, rebellions and demonstrations are examined as well as parades and festivals, the illegal as well as the legal. Apart from the American contrast of 'everyday' and 'new urbanism', however, there are still aspects with broader validity that can be applied to Europe as well. Temporary urbanism would be an alternative to urban planning by means of a master plan, a planning instrument of municipal governments that is of only limited applicability today: communes neither have the financial means nor the political power to plan entire neighbourhoods themselves. Like other individual actors, they have to proceed tactically rather than strategically, reacting to existing situations by attempting to locate the fulcrum that makes it possible to achieve large effects with limited means, by making arrangements with other actors or by cooperating with them. Here too interim use comes into play: master plans whose implementation dates are set far in the future because of legal proceedings and court battles open up a window of opportunity for temporary uses of their sites. When it is possible to produce long-term effects by means of such projects – for example, improving cultural capital by adding cultural projects – then they are more than just provisional.

The other side of temporary urbanism is the city of events: cities are increasingly wagering on cultural policies, rather than economic policies, to improve their chances in locational competition – in this case that means cultural events as part of the historic city, which are intended to make it more interesting for tourism and a well-heeled clientele – the so-called creative class. This leads to a homogenisation of the city centre and further displacement of functions to the periphery and hence also to a struggle over who can still use these homogenised spaces and who will be excluded – for example, low-income service workers who are supposed to provide the conveniences of the event city even though they themselves cannot take advantage of them. Another form of temporary urbanism takes part in this struggle, even though with insufficient resources, namely the self-proclaimed successors of the Situation-ists, the advocates of subversive visual politics, 'culture jamming' and the re-appropriation of public space by the public.

When one speaks of temporary urbanism, it is only a small step to concepts of social space, whether in the form of situational spaces for action, institutionalised regulations or normative territoria-lisations. In that context, and with an eye to the meaning of tem-porality for urban planning, one might think of the social space of temporary use as an instrument to dissolve or at least transform the other social space traditionally shaped by the urban-planning perspective, namely the deep-rooted social structure with its own identity and specific circumstances of urban space and economics and the associated problem-solving capacities. Temporary space in this sense would be not just a location of the reduced participation often found today, in which the affected parties are involved in the form of consultations, but rather a location where they can take control, if only for a short time and with a restricted scope of activity. The goal is a do-it-yourself attitude, rather than waiting for planners. It is just as much a cultural question as a social one. Temporary urbanism is, however, not merely a way to encourage participation; it also has tactical aspects. Temporary uses occupy a special place in the urban web: their small, short-lived interven-tions often lie under the threshold of perception and have a field of opportunities that is considerably larger than that of 'regular', long-term uses. On the other hand, despite their small size, they can sometimes develop a powerful effect that becomes significant for entire neighbourhoods. They can contribute to a city's develop-ment as 'bottom-up' planning instruments, as oppositional instru-ments to counter traditional urban planning from above, or they can find their place as a random project contrary to all planning, thus contributing to the complexity of the city. In contrast to master plans, they always permit a trial-and-error approach. They offer an opportunity to learn from initial steps and, if necessary, go back a little and set off on a different path. From the perspective of the transformation of urban space, that means that the uniform, homogenous neighbourhoods of the sort that result from master plans are extremely difficult to regenerate in later phases. Differences in cultural, social and economic structures make this easier. Such differences can be brought about with the help of temporary users. When encouraging temporariness, however, it must remain clear that the lasting effects should not be restricted to the micro-level.

Spaces, Places, Uses

What are these spaces, locations and uses that are defined by temporality? Temporary spaces are spaces opened up by temporary projects, whether they are produced by economic or aesthetic, urban planning, cultural reasons or simply by a desire to use something. Such spaces move first of all on the level of structures of action and interaction, of the production, use and appropriation of material spaces and, at least as importantly, on the level of systems of spatial representation. As part of the system of institutional regulation that mediates between spatial practice and material spaces, they are, perhaps, a rather new and unusual element. Here too, however, they have their effect and, as subversive practices, are also part of this system. They are located in specific places that are in turn part of material space as the physical substratum of social relationships. The choice of locations is in part random and in part deliberate, but it has specific effects on these places.

Locations of temporality are not Marc Augé's 'non-places': like Augé's 'places', they possess identity, relation and history. Unlike 'non-places', they are locations where temporary spaces have been constituted – projection surfaces. They are not empty; they are screens onto which something is projected, but they already contained information beforehand. They can be thought of as photosensitive material on which all the attempts at projection have left traces over time: immaterial palimpsests, so to speak, that nonetheless have a location. The intensity and durability of these traces varies. The question is: which actions can leave behind more enduring traces and how do the city's users become aware of these traces, perhaps resulting in networks of action. Even after the temporary use has ended, the location of temporality remains a projection screen onto which new projections can be made. The identity of this location is thus not fully determined; it can still be shaped. That is what attracts temporary users.

When viewed from a sufficient distance, any use is temporary. But we are talking about special use forms, and it is only one of their characteristics that they are viewed from the outset as limited in time – not necessarily by all those involved but perhaps by a property owner or the government, as opposed to the users. The unique aspect of temporary use in the sense it is employed here is thus not its provisional character but the idea of temporality inherent in it. This can be expressed, for example, in the fact that an event takes place in a particular location in order to charge it with a specific meaning it did not have previously, or that something is tried out, even though one isn't yet convinced it will function over the long term. It can take the form of a temporary aesthetic that seeks to distinguish a given use from a hegemonic culture, or it can try to postulate that there is a desire for use by the city's residents that is, perhaps, marginal and only short-term but nonetheless significant and worthy of attention. It can also indicate that there may be alternatives that lie between the old urban planning based on a master plan and abandoning all control in favour of the so-called market. It doesn't matter whether such use lasts an hour, a day, a month or ten years; what matters is the idea of temporality.

Bibliography

Amann, Marc, ed.
Go, Stop, Act! *Die Kunst des kreativen Straßenprotests;
Geschichte, Aktionen, Ideen* (Grafenau, 2004).

Arnstein, Sherry A.
'A Ladder of Citizen Participation.' *Journal of the American
Planning Association,* 35, no. 4 (1969), pp. 216–224.

Augé, Marc.
Non-Places: Introduction to an Anthropology of Supermodernity.
Translated by John Howe (London, 1995).

Becker, Jochen, ed.
*Bignes? Size Does Matter; Image/Politik; Städtisches Handeln;
Kritik der unternehmerischen Stadt* (Berlin, 2001).

Bittner, Regina, ed.
Die Stadt als Event: Zur Konstruktion urbaner Erlebnisräume
(Frankfurt am Main and New York, 2002).

Chase, John, John Kaliski and Margaret Crawford, eds.
Everyday Urbanism (New York, 1999).

Chi, Immanuel, Susanne Düchting, and Jens Schröter, eds.
Ephemer, temporär, provisorisch (Essen, 2002).

Fezer, Jesko, and Matthias Heyden.
*Hier entsteht: Strategien partizipativer Architektur und
räumlicher Aneignung* (Berlin, 2004).

Florida, Richard.
*The Rise of the Creative Class and How It's Transforming Work,
Leisure, Community and Everyday Life* (New York, 2004).

Florida, Richard.
Cities and the Creative Class (New York, 2005).

Gaebe, Wolf.
Urbane Räume (Stuttgart, 2004).

Häußermann, Hartmut, and Walter Siebel, eds.
Festivalisierung der Stadtpolitik: Stadtentwicklung durch große Projekte
(Opladen, 1993).

Kessl, Fabian, and Christian Reutlinger, Susanne Maurer, Oliver Frey, eds.
Handbuch Sozialraum (Wiesbaden, 2005).

Künstlerhaus Wien, Sønke Gau and Katharina Schlieben, eds.
Site-Seeing: Disneyfizierung der Städte? (Berlin, 2003).

Läpple, Dieter.
'Essay über den Raum: Für ein gesellschaftswissenschaftliches
Raumkonzept'. In Hartmut Häußermann et al., eds. *Stadt und Raum*
(Pfaffenweiler, 1991).

Lasn, Kalle.
Culture Jamming: The Uncooling of America (New York, 1999).

Mehrotra, Rahul, ed.
Everyday Urbanism: Margaret Crawford vs. Michael Speaks. Michigan
Debates on Urbanism 1 (Ann Arbor, 2005).

Ronneberger, Klaus, Stephan Lanz and Walther Jahn.
Die Stadt als Beute (Bonn, 1999).

Sewing, Werner.
Bildregie: Architektur zwischen Retrodesign und Eventkultur
(Basel, Boston, Berlin and Gütersloh, 2003).

StadtRat, ed.
Umkämpfte Räume (Hamburg, 1998).

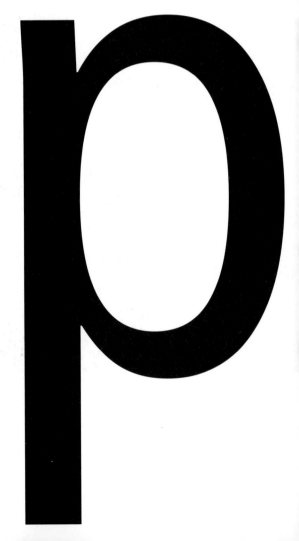

practice

ra

A Material that Never Comes to Rest
Concepts and Potentials of Temporary Spaces

The city, the trading centre of autonomy, embodies at every Florian Haydn moment of its life history an aggregate state, a material that never comes to rest. Its molecules are the people involved, the residents of the city. The energy the various aggregate states introduce is charged up by the constant, active search for possible open spaces. We are initiating an approach to the city both by way of the concept of urbanity and by an assessment of its current democratic potential. Space as a medium and agent of programmes forms the basis; programmed spaces with changing activities are temporary spaces.

The first basic idea is that of community: modernism's programmatic separation of functions led to the formation of mono-functional islands, especially on the outskirts of the city. It is possible to list the well-known advantages, but also grave disadvantages, such as a general segregation that leads to a loss of socialisation and community. For that reason, we focus the discussion of urbanity on the formation of community and its potential in terms of interpersonal, social, and informal interaction. A sustainable community is created by participatory decision-making processes. The intensity of the visibility or perceptibility of these processes in public or even semi-public space is a measure of the degree of urbanity. These processes necessitate structures for *negotiations*. The formation of such structures is supported by temporary spaces as building blocks of future programmes.

The second basic idea is that of public space: the urban lifestyle is characterised by an insurmountable diversity of overlapping and interpenetrating spaces that have been determined in various ways. The *boundaries* of spaces are not congruent with the built body of the city, but the drawing of these boundaries, which is achieved in different ways, does influence the body of the city. Within and along these social, legal, emotional, administrative, physical, topographic, and political boundaries, real living spaces are formed for individuals, territories between self-determined and heteronomous locations. Public space penetrates the built body of a city like a kind of meta-space, contained by the intersection of existing boundaries. Public space is not an objective fact. The boundaries of public space are constantly being constructed anew on the basis of negotiation and appropriation. Public space protects us from an excess of intimacy. Public space is a space of great anonymity. To put it another way, interpersonal contact takes place within partial public spaces. Partial public spaces are sometimes established in public space spontaneously and especially temporarily. The public sphere forms around concrete occasions, questions and objects.

The third basic idea is planning: the idea of urban planning – which is sometimes found even among the highest committees on the communal level – has thus far been based on locating buildings and connecting them to the local, national and international transport network as a way of improving their efficiency. Momentum is primarily sought by means of attracting new companies or by luring investors. Initiating complex, multi-layered but also small-scale extensions, whose high quality no one would dispute, is practically impossible. The much-criticised mono-functional concepts of modernism continue. The *programme* itself is secondary and interchangeable; the primary goal is positioning buildings. The genuine development of programmes is not the point at all. It marginalises the approach in which the programme is determined based on need with the support of strategic processes. The method generally applied is a signalling of need in the direction of the consumer by means of suggestive and aggressive advertising campaigns on the basis of image building and status symbols.

Using the examples of three realised projects, we will show how *negotiation, boundary* and *programme* relate to temporary spaces. The focus is on the potential that is produced when the community is reinforced, a public sphere is created and the programme development itself is connected with temporary spaces as part of the planning of architecture and urban development.

Sample Project for Negotiation: Conversations in purpose-built pavilions constructed from Euro pallets are intended to help get negotiations started where battlefronts had become emotionally charged and entrenched. All too often, it is clear that differences had been enflamed by media agitation and personal conversations had ceased. Emotionally charged enemies could in some cases truly be turned into rationally arguing opponents.[1]

Sample Project for Boundary: People sit down on the pavement, for example, or on a small square in the middle of a traffic island or somewhere else. What do they do there? They have breakfast, having brought stools and folding tables on which they place food. A small, autonomous space. Distributed throughout the urban region, sometimes simultaneously, they meet for breakfast and form a network of autonomous action. The temporary action of breakfast, in which all passers-by are welcome to participate, leaps over the functionally conceived space for action (pavement = walking) by means of this action of breakfasting in public and dissolves its boundaries using simple means like sitting.[2]

Sample Project for Programme: The space beneath a railway bridge is characterised by the meeting of various kinds of traffic: trams, cars, bicycles, trains, pedestrians and the underground. Several corridors exist side by side, separated by the piers of the

1 Wolfgang Zinggl, ed., *WochenKlausur: Gesellschaftspolitischer Aktivismus in der Kunst* (Vienna, 2001), p. 121ff.
2 See Permanent Breakfast in the project section of the present volume.

bridge. The piers are covered with 'wild' posters (i.e., with no permit), referring to locations and their programmes scattered throughout the city. In an analogy to the posters, a tarpaulin is spread between the piers. Like an oversized poster without reference to an event in the city, this spanned tarpaulin itself forms a space. A space on site behind the poster. The programme of the space is not defined, however, at the time it is created. The question arises: What will happen during its existence in this place. Memory and possibilities, as well as the memory of the possible, generate an interaction with the place and its surroundings.[3]

Temporary Spaces: The Urban Platform

By observing, we move within the spatial coordinates of a Central European city, which from the outside appears to be perfectly organised; its foundations are heroised only for models suited for image export. Proverbially, problems are pushed to the side and, whenever possible, removed entirely. The focus of the interest is on the city as *product*. Open *spaces for action* are sometimes edged out of central locations entirely in a process of progressive de-urbanisation. What are spaces for action? The sequence of different but connected processes realises an action. The programme is the abstraction, the structure, that makes it possible to repeat actions. The action is the experimental part, the attempt or test run, when establishing programmes. Open spaces for action per se make experiment possible. Spaces for action stand outside the capitalist logic of exploitation or demarcate their deficits. From the perspective of the public good, the city is involved in a permanent process of dispossession that is legitimised by capital transactions. Apart from these capital transactions, claims on the use of space

3 See Hirnsegel #7 (Brain-Sail #7) in the project section of the present volume.

are difficult to legitimate. 'As the cars increased, it was no longer possible to play in the street. Then zebra-crossings were established; people were happy they could at least cross the street safely. These are in essence constant processes of dispossession that we either do not notice at all or that we perceive as a profit, because it seems that something has been given back to us. [...] Walks in the city like zebra-crossings [...] should convey information in this sense; information about what we have lost.'[4] Alertly watching is the quietest way to participate in the shaping of spaces for action. The possibility of questioning programmes – that is, to open up new, different and better ones – characterises the democratic city. Temporality contains the essence of democracy. There are states that are constantly renewed, seeking decisions and creating moments of agreement. Actions, space for action and programme stand in the direct sequence in which the thematic temporary spaces actively intervene and propose concepts for the use of the city. The imagined temporary spaces create social knowledge and offer opportunities for active participation, rather than temporary spaces for an event-based leisure society.

Prototypes of Future Building Blocks for Programmes

Until now we have been describing the backgrounds, foundations and potential of temporary spaces as well as their significance in strengthening community in a democratic city. In what follows we will examine the roles involved in planning and attempt to clarify the respective boundaries of action. On what basis do architects develop buildings? What parameters do urban planners assume when developing an area? Who formulates the foundations? The market or speculation about how something should be? There are strategies that have been worked out to address specific target

4 Lucius Burckhardt, *Design = unsichtbar* (Ostfildern, 1995), p. 197.

71

groups. These target groups imply the demand the investor wants to satisfy. In the absence of alternative strategies, for example, everyone looking for housing is simply made part of the target group for inflexible housing projects. It seems that investors and communes who construct shared housing complexes are in agreement about this programme. No work is done on the side of 'demand', actually articulating the need; no support is offered. What would such support look like? In essence, a building is the fine adjustment of the future users' needs. The users' do not, however, formulate their needs. Depending on the ambition of the architects, who can assist in formulating needs, a 'house' prototype is developed via planning stages and then ultimately realised. The more the needs are put on the table, the more precisely and subtly the house can be developed on paper. One criterion of quality for an architect's work is how well the 'house' prototype realised can continue to be developed after it is built. That is to say, how well can the constructed space react to needs and ideas for use that were not known during the planning phase – for example, lifestyle changes in terms of career or living communities. Better still is when the building inspires the users to find new ways to use it. When planning a single apartment or home, there is usually an intimate trust between the planners and the users. Ideas for the need formulated grow thanks to synergetic inspiration. When entire neighbourhoods are being developed, it becomes necessary to pursue a different approach.

From the 'House' Prototype to the 'City' Prototype

We move from institutional administration to informal and participatory involvement in the design. Temporary uses should be equated with a kind of prototype that forms a point of departure for future, stable programmes. The current practice of urban planning is based entirely on the principle of supply and demand – or rather, on supply alone. Temporary uses can be understood as the demand itself. From the perspective of planners and communes involved in planning, this means a step in the direction of the residents, who become participants in the planning of the city through their active involvement in temporary uses. Initiating and supporting temporary uses is part of a new, alternative practice of urban planning that creates potential space by means of experimental demand. This new urban planning no longer views space exclusively in terms of its physical boundaries but also recognises 'intelligent' space, which by means of the indifference of its internal organisation stimulates and reveals opportunities for using the city. A perpetual transformation process accompanies us through time. The creation of such spaces depends on experimenting with cause and effect. The vision consists in establishing complex particles of space here and there in the cityscape in order to explore fundamental possibilities for social development. The theory of the temporary space seems to be in contradiction to its archaic roots, which saw space as something stable, powerful and enduring. The temporary space, in contrast to the functionally predetermined space, leads to other results in its use. The way that planning assigns functions to spaces has been called into question. From now own, use stands for spatial thinking; space for thought per se is reality. That means we are practicing something that was previously unimaginable. Use itself exists in time before its shell: the building. Therein, at least, lies one relevant potential to be ascribed to temporary spaces. On the other hand, we might conclude, following Buckminster Fuller: 'We must put all the resources of the world into a fluid, fluctuating, mobile state so that nothing exists that we have to try to get rid of.'[5]

5 John Cage, For the Birds (London, 1984), 61.

Urban Intelligence

The use of buildings and urban areas is subject to cycles of up- Mirko Pogoreutz
and downturns, in the course of which there are sometimes moments of transition, of uncertainty and of standstill. If the former
uses have already been abandoned but either new programmes
are not on the horizon or plans could not be implemented, then
there are gaps in utilization – urban open spaces in which frequently new, innovative uses are located briefly. In these temporary spaces, actors and players emerge who are otherwise under-
represented in the city. Temporary users are often pioneers, in
terms of both space and programme. They develop new, experimental programmes for spaces used and bring new life to urban
regions. Because the sums they need to invest for their uses are
lower, they are more likely to risk the failure of a given programme;
this also opens up a greater potential for successful possibilities.
Their reinterpretations of the existing and their approach to found
objects often prepares the ground for the re-urbanisation of municipal territories and even to serve as a model for developing other
regions, to which their new, successful programmes can be trans-
ferred. The attendant circumstances of temporary uses and their
potential role in the development of a city long went unexamined.
From 2001 to 2003, the international, interdisciplinary research
project Urban Catalyst examined strategies for temporary uses in
five European metropolises: Berlin, Amsterdam, Naples, Vienna
and Helsinki. It was initiated by Philipp Oswalt and Klaus Overmeyer in Berlin, directed in cooperation with Philipp Misselwitz
and co-financed by the European Union as part of the fifth supporting programme of Key Action 4: The City of Tomorrow and
Cultural Heritage. With the Studio Urban Catalyst at the Tech-

nische Universität Berlin as co-ordinator, a dozen project partners explored the causes and foundations of current historical temporary uses and their potential for urban transformation processes. In addition to case studies, a central concern was to establish temporary uses in so-called test areas or to follow them actively. In addition to the communal administrations of Vienna, Berlin and Amsterdam Noord, architects, sociologist and lawyers participated.[1]

Residual Spaces

If one follows Rem Koolhaas, the distinction between public and private space has become obsolete, and it is better to speak of controlled and abandoned residual spaces. If the phenomenon of temporary uses is viewed from the perspective of Berlin, it also becomes evident that Berlin was particularly well suited to a study of residuals 'because in the last fifteen years, as a consequence of its many unutilized areas, it was a kind of urban laboratory for exploring residuals.'[2] One could say that during the 1990s temporary uses found their habitat in Berlin after the fall of the Wall. From these Berlin experiences and the consequences of the economic and fiscal crisis, which is also a crisis of urban planning, the fundamental working thesis of Urban Catalyst concluded that it is time to explore what potential temporary uses have for urban

1 Final Report of Magistratsabeilung 18 – Stadtentwicklung und Stadtplanung of the city of Vienna on the European Union research project 'Urban Catalyst: Strategien für temporäre Nutzungen; Entwicklungspotentiale für urbane Residualflächen in europäischen Metropolen', published in *Werkstattberichte,* no. 60, ed. Stadtplanung Wien, Magistratsabteilung 18, Vienna, 2003.
2 Philipp Oswalt and Rudolf Stegers, *Berlin: Stadt ohne Form; Strategien einer anderen Architektur* (Munich and New York, 2000).

development and what would be necessary to employ them effectively. It is first necessary to determine, however, what significance temporary uses can retain when the pressure on use is higher than it was in a Berlin with a vacant centre.

Homo Ludens versus Homo Oeconomicus

The sample projects collected in this volume demonstrate the diversity of approaches that can be collected under the rubric of temporary use. Temporary is a term that is difficult to define; ultimately, all urban uses are limited in time, and an increasing number of uses exist for increasingly shorter periods. If the point is to examine the potential for temporary uses in urban development, the extent to which they can be instrumentalised for planning, it seems necessary to formulate the object of study more precisely: what does an urban planner or resident mean by temporary uses? In Urban Catalyst, temporary uses were interpreted as interim uses. Interim uses can be thought of as a subset of temporary uses but also as an alternative model. They refer to a conscious anteriority and posteriority, a prior past and an imagined future. They already contain an 'in order to'; use is placed in a relationship and a function is attributed to it. It is an interim use only in reference to the special character of the prior and subsequent use. Temporary uses are supply-oriented; interim uses are demand-oriented. Then there is something I would like to call the end in itself of temporary uses: one might say that temporary uses are limited in time of their own accord, whereas interim uses are limited from outside, by planning that aims at other goals. Interim uses can be planned; temporary uses, scarcely at all. Temporary uses are a game – a game that questions the current culture of urban planning, with whose help it becomes possible to depart from the well-worn paths of urban planning, and also a game in a position to reinterpret urbanity because it is critical of rituals. Its productivity for the city and for urban society can only become clear to us when temporary uses have left their current niche. But that does not depend on them alone.

Vienna

In contrast to Berlin, Vienna has not been affected by shrinking and long-term de-industrialisation. On the contrary, in the wake of the political changes in Eastern Europe and with the entry of the central Eastern European countries into the European Union, Vienna has moved from the edge to the centre. Vienna thus lacks the incomparable breeding ground for temporary activities that Berlin has. There are few unutilised urban areas here; where they do exist, new plans for them are quickly presented. Nevertheless, or precisely for that reason, Vienna has many small examples of temporary uses and a tradition of actionist urban exploration that dates back to the 1960s. Important practical experiences with cultural interim uses could be gained during the transformation of the former cable factory (KDAG) into a new section of the city and by the interim use of the present museum district in the centre of the city. In the latter case, there is also the question of how temporary uses could be made permanent: thanks to their work countless small cultural initiatives accumulated cultural capital in this location that was ultimately taken over along with the site by the 'main users' from the world of high culture after the area was reconstructed, while most of the small users had to leave.

After several failed attempts by the Vienna team of Urban Catalyst to establish a test area in the city, it was decided that it was appropriate in Vienna to work on basic information and networking for temporary uses and spread the word to potential temporary users about the potential of temporary uses and the existing opportunities for such in Vienna. In Vienna in particular, however, the involuntary side of temporary uses became evident: then they are suddenly no longer voluntary, short-term interventions but rather the only substitute for long-term practices not available to a marginalised scene. In 2003, following Urban Catalyst, the symposium 'tempo..rar: Temporäre Nutzungen im Stadtraum' took property owners, city planners, temporary users and scholars on a four-part walking tour of empty buildings in Vienna and encouraged interchange among them, which revealed common interests but above all many fundamental differences.

Summary

There are a large number of urban activities and functions that independently develop parameters for their own 'urban planning from below' and that look after urban problem areas themselves without being officially authorised or recognised tools of communal urban planning. By documenting case studies and actively accompanying interim uses, Urban Catalyst succeeded in encouraging coming to terms with the temporary and reinforcing an awareness that temporary uses have not played a role in urban planning that is in keeping with their potential. By concentrating on interim uses, however, certain aspects of temporary uses remain unexplored, namely those that do not function as means to urban development ends. These include issues of informal, spontaneous, alternative self-organisation, whose primary characteristic is the use of available urban, programmatic, economic open spaces, but that also have other features that make them perfectly compatible with the neo-liberal economy, from shifting risk to individuals to accelerating the use of space. Even within the context of functionality for urban development, however, interim uses frequently enough play a precarious role in gentrification processes. In such temporary uses as an end to themselves or as ways out, dynamics and efficiencies develop that cannot be planned. Employing temporary uses as strategic tools also means turning them into economic instruments, even though they have been precisely a means of those who do not participate in urban planning decisions and could continue to do so – consider squatting, for example. It must therefore become a task of municipal politics to keep open spaces for such unplanned, spontaneous urban articulation. Temporary uses are extremely political, as a result of their inherent element of self-organisation. If they are used more frequently, further researched and developed, it will become possible to redefine participation in the city. Projects like Urban Catalyst that research on the margins of official forms of architecture – a discipline whose task ultimately largely still consists in designing new material shells for space – naturally question the role of architects and make it possible for them to expand their perspective on the subject of their work. Architects, who are normally the addressees of others' commissions, programmes and problems, find in temporary uses solutions for urban problems by means other than architectural or design interventions communicated in abstract plans. Thinking through temporary uses in planning or designing outside of planning makes it possible, on the one hand, to interact more directly with the city and to become an urban actor. Urban intelligence and creativity are employed in an immediate, concrete urbanism.[3] On the other hand, they can in turn have an effect on the established practice of architectural planning and draw greater attention to the consideration of and orientation towards social spaces as a way of changing such practice with lasting effect.

3 I wish to thank Oliver Frey of the Institut der Soziologie für Raumplanung und Architektur, Technische Universität Wien, for inspiring discussions on concrete urbanism.

Spaces for Action and for Laughing Too
On the Public Effect of Participation in Urban Spaces

A Meeting Place for People in the Rice Villages

An artist gets into her car and drives from the big city to a small Elke Krasny mountain village. Her car is full of stones. She will get them to speak. The artist's name is Hiroko Inoue. Her destination is one of Japan's most important rice growing regions. Rural beauty, economic crisis and population loss characterise the region's six communities, including the city of Tokamachi and the village of Nakasato. Since 1994 another form of development has opened up for the Echigo-Tsumari region: the Art Necklace Project. A proposal for an international art garden for a triennial combined with the idea of investing in the landscape, in the form of streets, parks and cottages. The guests are not only internationally active artists but also, and primarily, tourists. Although Fram Kitagawa, the general director of the Echigo-Tsumari Triennial, had set the goal that artists should grapple with the particular circumstances and needs of the locals, this approach needs time for an understanding to develop. Hiroko Inoue did not want to create a traditional sculpture. She packed her stones into her car, went from house to house knocking on doors and engaged the people in conversation. Frequently she was invited in, for tea or food. Many said they were willing to comply with her wish. They were supposed to write on the stone the name of the person who was most important to them, who was closest to their heart. Inoue met many older married couples there; often the name was written on the stone in secret. It wasn't always the spouse's name. The artist herself added a name, that of her father. All the stones together now form a monument; the work from 2003 is called *Memory – Regeneration.*

A collective recalls its loved ones, its most important people. The names are on the bottom of the stones, protected from prying eyes; someday they will disappear. What remains are the memories. Together, the stones form an oval. The stone oval is surrounded by chairs, on which one can sit and meditate, on life and death. It is a place where the most private things remain private and yet it creates a public space. A sculptural site of meditative observation, a poetic place for participation, where memories remain intangible and yet palpable for all who participated.

Designing a Square in a Small City

In the spring of 2000 a group of artists were asked for advice. An old public square was to be given a new look. Change can lead to discord in a city. WochenKlausur – Elisabeth Eitelberger, Pascale Jeannée, Carola Stabauer, Stephan Szigetvary and Wolfgang Zinggl – had six weeks to activate the potential of citizen involvement on Pfarrplatz in Krems. The strategic use of time as a resource is essential to WochenKlausur's precise way of taking action. The rules for citizen involvement in Krems were both simple and rigorous. The citizens who had participated in the information and discussion events were allowed to join the working groups. There was a poll. The questions were not primarily of a formal nature – what should it look like – but rather of a structural nature: what should the square permit the users to do, what should be put in it, what should be permitted or prohibited. Questionnaires were filled out by 219 citizens. An additional 47 interviews were conducted with individual residents: shopkeepers, business owners, representatives of the parish, local politicians. Experts provided input on the architecture, the traffic situation, the city's history and the process of citizen involvement. The two working groups had a 3-D model available. A consensus always had to be reached. The result was democratic, but not in a glossy tabloid version, rather in the

sense of involvement in civil society. It was the ideas of those who showed their commitment to the redesign of Pfarrplatz and who invested a great deal of their time who mattered and became part of the solution. It was not simply about taking a vote, which would only mean disappointment. Rather, it was about how important a place is, how much commitment is worth and the fact that participation makes a difference. The model shows a lot of promise; the question whether this kind of decision-making process really does make a difference when it comes to *realpolitik* depends on the particular case.

The Founding of a City between Reality and Utopia

The AugartenStadt cannot be found on any map. But it refers to real places in Vienna: Wallensteinplatz, the Augarten, Gaußplatz. A project to redesign Wallensteinplatz using public participation came to nothing. As a result, two urban planners, Uschi and Dieter Schreiber of Aktionradius Augarten, started a move out of the real city by founding their own. The main square of the new city would be the contested Wallensteinplatz. It was not just the redesign that gave cause to reflect, but also, and above all, the name. Is it right to name a city square after a war hero of this calibre in the age of Saddam Hussein or George Bush? That is the question considered by the Augartenstadt. Renamings mark times of crisis and ideological changes. After the Second World War, tentatively at first, there was a 'de-Nazification' of public space. Streets, squares and alleys were renamed. After the end of socialism in the former Eastern Bloc countries, there was a similar purging process of urban space as a space of memories. The interesting thing in the case of Wallensteinplatz is that it is a question of a *longue durée*. A name that was seemingly sacrosanct historically is currently being confronted with its history. The fictive-utopian AugartenStadt began to unfold its real potential and sent a delegation to Magdeburg to apologise. On 20 May 1631, Magdeburg was completely destroyed by the emperor's army, led by General Wallenstein. Thereafter ravages on that scale were called Magdeburgisations. A special kind of partnership between the two cities was forged. The AugartenStadt and the City of Magdeburg submitted a joint project to the European Union. Uschi Schreiber of Aktionsradius Augarten signed the application as the City Councilwoman for Spaces and Dreams. Secretly, everyone was hoping to discuss with the EU the reasons for the rejection. But the EU surprised everyone by approving the application. On 20 May 2005, the city apologised to Magdeburg. At the *Tschuidigung Magdeburg* celebration on Wallensteinplatz, relations between the former enemies were normalised. The Magdeburg delegation presented an official greeting from the mayor offering an invitation in return and gifts for the hosts. The AugartenStadt follows the principle of the urban revolt from below, not above. Large public celebrations exploring the potential of the space are characteristic of the very idea of idea of the AugartenStadt, thus coming to terms with spaces drenched with power and instilled with the burden of a historical legacy.

Ascent for the Gaze from Above onto One's Own Responsibility

From 18 June to 31 July 2005, a temporary vertical playing field was located on Wallensteinplatz in Vienna's twentieth district. Twenty metres tall, it was a hybrid of architecture, installation and sculpture that was not only usable but was also inhabited by artists and architecture students. The seductive promise of usability was taken literally above all by the children and young people around the square whose vacations had just begun; from morning to evening, they climbed 'their' tower. This physical use was much greater and more intense than the architects who initiated the project – Peter Fattinger, Veronika Orso and Michael Rieper – had expected. They were simply astonished by the intensity with which children and young people participated. The project's title – add on – suggested adding one's own things, though that was not intended in the design. The pleasure of the discoverers overcame inhibitions; old people, young people, people from the neighbourhood, people from other parts of the city with an interest in culture – all met in the city tower, with an intensity heightened by the time limit. Aesthetically, physically, one's own place became someone else's place in order to become that much more one's own.

The Stranger in One's Own Home

An artist enters the airplane. Thirty black neutral objects accompany her on her journey from Austria to Canada. Gertrude Moser-Wagner knew that she wanted to communicate with the people at her destination, Durham. The small Canadian city has 26,000 residents. Everywhere the lawns in the front yards were flawless, excessively well tended with nobody to be seen, but with the Canadian flag flying above them. That made her think. The rules of Moser-Wagner's game are conceptual. Those who are invited to participate must have something to do with the city's name. She found in the phonebook all the residents whose last names began with D, U, R, H, A or M. She delivered the 327 letters personally. And everyone was asked to photograph the black object 'inside and outside the home' with the enclosed disposable camera. The strange guest, originally purchased at IKEA, remained with the participants. In exchange, the resulting photographs became the artist's property. An art game with rules and latitude of one's own interpretations. Wheelchairs, crystal dishes, plants, people, interiors and exteriors were photographed together with the catalyst. The artist created a Durham tableau from the photographs, and it was presented in the local gallery. Observing a restricted place, accompanied by a strange object, gave insights into one's own life and that of others, and it opened the eyes not only of the artist

but also of the residents of Durham to what is important in the homes of twenty-four residents of their city.

Home Is More Than One's Own Four Walls

Seventeen art teachers ask questions. They set out to get to know the community. Each of them looks for two people to interview. And what is more obvious than one's own house, home in the metaphorical sense. What does home mean to you? How did you get there? What object best represents your idea of home? This community art project was led by Jonathan Silverman, who teaches art education at Saint Michael's College in Colchester, Vermont. Art education that temporarily leaves the classroom, finds the common denominator of a current visual culture and turns familiar things at home into a question. A reflection on perceiving one's own things differently as a result of others' questions. Fifth-generation Vermonters were asked as well as a Sudanese refugee, a teenager living in a youth centre and retired shop owners. The objective answers of the participants became something mobile. Then they encountered the public, presented in the Fletcher Free Library in Burlington, Vermont, in July 2005.

A Neighbourhood Is Modernised

An old working-class district of The Hague is in the middle of an urbanisation process. Near the city centre lies Transvaal, one of the poorest areas in The Netherlands. Three-quarters of the 17,000 people living here come from outside The Netherlands. This neighbourhood is undergoing an urban-development transformation. Change is improvement, change is loss, loss of the familiar, loss of affordable housing. Three thousand homes are razed to make room for 1,600 new, expensive housing units. The mobiel projectbureau OpTrek – the artists Sabrina Lindemann and Annechien

Meier – followed this urban transformation as eyewitnesses for a three-year period beginning in 2002. Being an eyewitness means more than distanced observation; it means having a debate with the people living here about what is happening to their living space. Interview-portraits, intercultural cooking for a day in the Restaurant Gratis or an online photo archive that combines images of the city with personal family photos… The investigation of the complex and conflictual process was pursued together with international artists and artists' groups and penetrated deep into the local problems but also sought to reflect in a way that extended to the general.

Spontaneous Action on the Street

Three brides walk down the street. They are accompanied by a man dressed in black. He speaks to passers-by, politely and encouragingly, asking if they wouldn't like to have their picture taken with them. The photographs are collected in a book, and everyone who participated gets a copy. Brides ensure emotional attentiveness. A bus drives past, with the driver's door open. One of the three sirens asks him for a note. Somewhat hesitantly, he offers a dark 'Aaaahhhh', which the sirens take as the starting point for some improvised singing. Three women in strangely old-fashioned clothing sit down in Café Jelinek in Vienna's sixth district. Right away a conversation starts up with the women at the next table. In the Café Sperl the waiters and guests are asked to sing. The Polish waiter sings 'Maja the Bee'; the writer Robert Menasse is serenaded. The sirens – the music therapist Barbara Gabriel, the art teacher Susanna Gruber and the 'cultural mediator' Gabriele Stöger – intervene spontaneously, laughing and singing in public. They don't sing from sheet music but they do sing in many genres, ranging from opera to atonal Christmas songs. They were accompanied on their 'sixth odyssey with a brief halt on Naxos' by the composer Richard V. Strauss. These actions in summer 2005 were part of a larger project, Der 6te Sinn (The Sixth Sense), a participatory networking project in the sixth district, based on socio-cultural partnerships. The meeting between the sirens and Richard V. Strauss provided some stimuli. Words were exchanged; people began to laugh; a few bars were hummed. Thus, for a brief moment, what is generally understood in the philosophical discourse as the 'public sphere' touches with the physical public space of the street. For a brief time, something shared is produced in the encounter.

Reflections on Giving and Taking in a Game with Rules

Participation is a game with rules. By means of the production of shared 'locations', in the literal and metaphorical senses, new spaces are created: spaces for thinking; spaces for imagining; spaces for experiencing; concrete, physically tangible spaces. Participatory action means interrupting the everyday. Routines are repealed. And yet it is precisely the everyday or familiar that can become an object of observation. By means of this displacement, the figure of the alien that places itself between one's own things and their perception, processes are set in motion. In this displacement there is a potential for another form of urban action and another state of being, both as subjects and as a community. The more limited the place of action, the more precise the interaction and involvement. Seeing oneself in a new light, reflecting on one's own surroundings, placing oneself in a different relationship to other people and the city. When one's behaviour is prodded to make a change in one's own relationships, the participatory aspect evokes possibilities. The clearer the rules, the more precise the methods, the more surprising the forms of participation. The city is visual material. Making it that requires artistic, urbanistic or architectonic intervention. The dramaturgical trick of visualising one's own qualities by way of the figure of the alien liberates the potential for reflection in participatory action. The less time is available, the more intense the interaction becomes. The more limited the venue, the more interesting the changes in perception. The initial stages of participatory action can be diverse in nature, conceptual, democratic, creative, interpersonal, formal, critical of society. Often the fields overlap. Points of departure, objectives and results often speak different languages. But the urban artistic dramaturgy of intervention, of emerging, of doing and of disappearing demarcates precisely the present crisis. Understanding one's surroundings as one's own, making them one's own, is not so easy. Paradoxically, participation produces a share not so much in artistic action but rather in one's own living environment, in one's own life context, in one's own urban space. The formats of the action seem to be quite simple: giving and taking, asking and answering, looking and looking again. Yet in the precise positing of the respective approaches, events are produced that shift perception and allow action to speak and take form. Whether ephemeral or more enduring, through the act of participation people become part of the artistic production, of urban action. And the artistic labour – the work or the event – becomes part of them. That means change.

For conversations and information, I am grateful to Hiroko Inoue, Wolfgang Zinggl, Dieter Schreiber, Peter Fattinger, Gertrude Moser-Wager, Jonathan Silverman, Sabrina Lindemann and Gabriele Stöger.

desire

de

X: Then it was gone. He had resolved to reduce his consumption of cigarettes again. But until the next one comes?! The interval was too short for a whole cigarette… but it was too long just to stand around. According to the schedule, it was supposed to appear within the next four minutes. If not for the experience that in Vienna schedules are a law that cannot be respected out of a sense of tradition: probably a combination of regulations concerning fare agreements and an attempt to emphasise the humanness of public transport. He had always wondered whether the display of arrival times in the underground was manually controlled. Usually minutes six to two would pass more or less synchronously with the usual measurement of time – like I said: more or less. Sometimes it happened that the minutes passed at 30-second intervals. Only the last minute often took two to three minutes to pass. He thought of Beckett: Vladimir: 'Time has stopped.' And Estragon's reply only comes twenty pages later: 'Perhaps it has stopped.' But Estragon did not mean time, only his watch. The idea that the public transport in Vienna interprets its lawless scheduling philosophically makes it easier to wait. In order to put out his positive view of this attitude, he decided to have a cigarette anyway, even at the risk he would have to put it out before finishing it. Paradox: you can say either 'put out an idea' or 'put out a cigarette'. He imagined encountering the following sentence in the rules of the Viennese public transport system: 'Smoking is prohibited in the stations. Please articulate your cigarette before entering the station. Violations are punishable.' The fact that his violation was not an isolated incident reassured him: the collective as protective mechanism, even if this collective was not a collective in the strict

Büro für kognitiven Urbanismus

Andreas Spiegl,
Christian Teckert

sense but just a random collection of those who had arrived too early or too late. The distances maintained to others waiting was the product of imaginary personal borders: social conventions that contradicted the laws of the distribution of elements in gaseous states and ensured that the distances themselves were maintained even as pressure increased and distance decreased in the equilibrium. The exceptions proved the rule: one bloke was headed on a collision course, only to slip past just before the moment of impact – in shirtsleeves, eyes straight ahead, unfriendly. The realisation that this passenger would use a different entrance vaporised the rising contempt. A last glance.

The lawless two minutes had started. Slowly, the initially empty space began to be populated. Several people strolled along an imaginary figure in space; others swayed in place. Those who had not brought along a partner for conversation or chanced to run into one had to remain silent. The inevitable communication was limited to the visual, to sizing up by eye. He remembered a film: *Run, Lola, Run.* Lousy film, lousy title. Only the speeded-up accounts of the biographies of random passers-by was worth the time. Behind each figure one sensed a story through the quotidian. 'Monodrama' was what Stan Douglas called such episodes. And it was also Stan Douglas who advocated Beckett's films. Douglas, Beckett – Beckett Proust Douglas. Douglas also had a passage from *Remembrance of Things Past* read over a loop of a train journey: a circular narrative in which two motifs from the nineteenth century were linked. Time has stopped. Only the watch keeps going. The watch does not recognise the repetition it practices. With a similar riddle, Eddie Constantine as Lemmy Caution, undercover as Ivan Johnson, outsmarts the control of Alpha 60 in Jean-Luc Godard's *Alphaville.* Standing in front of him was someone who reminded him of Eddie Constantine. He also thought of Natasha von Braun, but there was no one who resembled her among those waiting. The shape of the Praterstern, with its circular traffic, followed the structure of *Alphaville,* which was also circular. The film begins with a scene in which Eddie Constantine lights a cigarette in his Ford Galaxy, as he leaves the Outerlands to travel into the city he will destroy. Only the light of the cigarette illuminates his face. A hero, illuminated. A linear narrative is introduced to destroy the circular one. His cigarette was half finished, and he was thinking that today the linear has become a problem. The countdown. Another minute left.

What surprised him was the wild mixture of those waiting, who for whatever reasons found themselves together for a view minutes, encountering one another, getting out of one another's way. The platform reminded him of an egg timer: the area provides a broad spectrum of the most heterogeneous directions and figures who then collect on the platform, become more numerous, climb aboard and then disperse again into the city along the route. A temporary urban space. In contrast to other spaces dedicated to a function or interest, which do indeed suggest a collective desire, this space was a disinterested one. To speak of disinterested pleasure would be going too far; 'disinterested interest' would be more appropriate. The only common desire was to get away – a space that is not there: a somewhere, an elsewhere. The platform was a space that only represented a space of time, a temporary use that promised another space. Its spatial selflessness enabled it to view the city – its heterogeneity, its unimportant things and boundaries, knowing that these phenomena would no longer play a role at the moment of departure. In a few seconds this room would be empty again, only to fill up anew. Again and again, but not in the same way. An urban variable. Most of the heads were turned in the direction from which it was supposed to come.

Y: He couldn't believe it. Until now, it had always worked at the last minute. He still remembered the words of the woman at the airline counter: 'Sorry, the gate closed five minutes ago; we cannot let you pass.' She told him the next flight to his destination was the following day and asked whether she should make a reservation. He looked at the electronic display board; his plane was no longer on it. He had to sit down for a minute to smoke a cigarette and consider his options. He had fallen into a time hole: not really here any longer, but no opportunity to be there anytime soon.

He looked around. Bustling activity dominated everyone; a space consisting of directional vectors and lines of movement. He couldn't help but think of Robert Musil's remark in *The Man without Qualities* that cities could be recognised by their walk, by the way the movement in the streets swings. But here, unlike before at the Praterstern, it no longer seemed possible to recognize anything specifically Viennese about the movements. The idea that, despite having missed his plane, he was still somewhere other than Vienna, comforted him.

Many of the people around him were waiting, but here the waiting was very different. It was more goal-oriented: a logical part of a continuous movement from here to there. He felt alien among them, displaced. Really he should have taken the next bus back into the city, but he began to play with the idea of settling into his time hole. His friends in the city assumed he was already on his way to his native city, but no one was waiting for him there. He felt like one of the figures in the film *Paris qui dort* by René Clair, in which all movements in the city were frozen for a day, apart from the protagonists in the film, who were sitting in an airplane at the time. Except now he was the calm pole amid all the movements. But precisely this other form of waiting, this displaced temporality, enabled him to see the space that was distinguished by the fact that it should be perceived as little as possible. It was supposed to function as a 'time space', as an interstitial zone, as a commodified space, as a space in which the travellers themselves became commodities. But now he felt excluded from the effortless circulation of commodities and transported to a transitional time space.

It made him think of all the terms applied to such places: transit spaces, non-locations, non-places... as if they all lacked something. But the spaces were filled with different speeds and times, with temporalities, full of desire for other places, with memories of other spaces. He had the impression that the disparateness of the architecture around him was a silent admission of overpowering temporalities that could no longer simply represent the space and dared to be translated into architectural language.

He grew uneasy. It was as if someone in the crowd of waiting people was observing him, had recognised him. A moment ago he had felt invisible, as the centre of the world but at the same time hidden from the world. Like a *flâneur* in nineteenth-century Paris. Now he felt more like a voyeur; in this place, his waiting and his gaze no longer had the function he attributed to them. In a strange way, he felt he was being watched. When the space became visible to him as a transitional time space, he also became more visible for the space. The initial joy he had felt at the idea of settling in to his dislocation, using it as a mode of perception, made him suspicious that his other temporality made him visible.

He decided not to ride back into the city, but rather to look for a hotel near the airport. The room looked like he had expected. The usual worldwide standard. That connected it to every possible other place. As in Howard Hughes' residences where, despite their location, the same food was served, so as to spare him unpleasant surprises. Spaces in permanent latency. Waiting rooms... white bed sheets, white handkerchiefs, white curtains, white walls... they seemed like canvases placed in the rooms... blank canvases that were just waiting to become projection screens for a moment, only to be washed clean again the next day. He suspected that the traces of desire must still be somehow visible in the white surfaces, communicating to him a sense of security.

He turned the television on and flipped through the channels. Since television programming began broadcasting twenty-four hours a day, it has become a kind of parallel city, he thought. A city that was present everywhere in the world, permanent simultaneity. Images in a holding pattern, waiting to be brought to life by the remote control. He stopped at Monica Vitti's face. One channel was showing *L'Avventura* by Michelangelo Antonioni. A group of friends looking for Anna, who had suddenly disappeared on an island excursion. People in empty spaces and desolate landscapes. Waiting… for Anna… waiting for the lost congruence of time and space… waiting for the as yet redeemed promise of modernity. Once again he felt watched, addressed: from the pre-future – as it will have been, when he will have arrived again in the course of time.

Footnotes

In this essay we have outlined an idea of the temporary that views the temporary and interim use of empty or available spaces not so much as an experimental prototype for a longer-term use but sees it in temporality, in a limited span of time, even in features of a spatial and urban quality. If temporary uses of seemingly unused spaces are considered primarily a field for experimentation, in order to select from the results only those projects that can be transformed into long-term undertakings, then temporality is conceived negatively from the outset: as a test run that needs to be completed as quickly as possible so that one can focus on stabilisation and codification again. Experience shows that many projects only become possible because they were temporary – and fell into crisis at the very moment they, as something temporary, were supposed to lead the way to the institutional. A mere reference to the history of the former 'alternative spaces' or 'off spaces' of the early 1990s should suffice here. If temporality is seen as merely the run-up to longer-term solutions, then this perspective already implies it is inscribed into a logic of preservation that affects not only the necessary infrastructure but also the nature of a project. Paradigmatic of this logic is an appeal to the so-called niche economy, which recognises in the smart and subsidised experiment only the future of a viable and expanding market, following the slogan: today's experiment is tomorrow's future.

Temporality as a prototypical phenomenon tends to counteract temporality itself. The political expression of this negative conception of temporality takes the form of excluding the very desires that are justified only as a passing phenomenon. The temporary has not rights; it has to cede to a right that claims longevity. If temporary use is seen as merely the prototype for a long-term utilisation, then the plea for the temporary runs the risk of inadvertently demanding a right of asylum from the temporary: here too an allusion to the current political discussion of asylum rights and their future should suffice. The conception of an empty or unused space as economic fallow land is the product of a logic of exploitation that defines it as unused capital. The principle behind it, however, is based on an idea of functionality that sees only uselessness in the dysfunctionality of the unused and empty. A good idea for useless spaces fills their vacancy with functionality. This annuls the functionality of vacancy and undeclared use of available spaces. Temporary functionalisation of empty spaces in the spirit of a prototypical presentation turns against the function of the temporary that it seeks to overcome. Using the example of waiting in the city, the Büro für kognitiven Urbanismus addressed spaces that enable a specific look at urban space by means of the temporary time space of waiting. Waiting itself is one example of these times spaces that are successively decreased or cut. Waiting represents a temporary space that previously lay between two functional time spaces. In order to functionalise unused and empty waiting in a way analogous to empty spaces, an infrastructure has been developed in recent years that eliminates waiting in order to gain attention. This attention once again guides the gaze according to a regime of the logic of exploitation. The useless gaze of the waiting and their dysfunctional perception are reconfigured. The attraction of the urban is exchanged for an image of the urban. What could be seen in these temporary and unused time spaces is not seen because something can be seen. Questions that could be asked are not asked because questions are asked. These waiting rooms, temporary and empty rooms, were previously an outlet through which the functional attention could evaporate into an attention to the dysfunctional. With the disappearance of these temporary empty spaces, the attention to the dysfunctional is also lost.

Horror Vacui

Permanent Breakfast is a game, an art project, art in a public space Ursula Hofbauer, Friedemann Derschmidt and public art, but also urban planning or a social project or a tool to test the quality of public spaces or, to put it another way, to ensure the public character of a certain space.

The game is begun when one or more people set up a breakfast table in a square, a street location or other public open space, offering, for example, coffee, rolls and jam and inviting passers-by to join them for breakfast. In the familiar, simple manner of a chain letter, the breakfasters are asked to organise a similar public breakfast the next day and invite the passers-by in turn. Ideally, everyone who organises the breakfast should invite at least four people, so that on the second day there are already sixteen, on the third day sixty-four and on the tenth day over a million people having breakfast in public.

Permanent Breakfast is renewed every year with a kick-off breakfast in Vienna's city centre. The goal of this initiation event is to invite as many people as possible to disseminate the game of a public breakfast over the course of the year: everywhere in the city but also beyond the municipal and national borders. In the ten years of its existence, the project has spread in the manner of a chain letter and taken root in most of the European metropolises. We ask all the breakfasters to send photos of their breakfasts, if possible. We have received hundreds of such reports back by mail, from nearly all the large cities of Europe but also from New York, Taiwan and the South Seas.

As a rule, the reactions to the public breakfast are positive. Passers-by readily sit down, drink coffee and chat. Even tourists and older people, who might at first be thought to have stricter ideas of order, overcame such behaviour. Many of them were probably appropriating some public space for their own objectives and needs for the first time. It helps that breakfasting is as harmless an activity as could be. No one would think it could be a kind of political rally, and yet public breakfasts are that as well: assemblies for the purpose of debate and exchange of opinions. The right to hold such assemblies – even without prior notification – has been guaranteed under German and Austrian law, for example, by their respective constitutional courts. That means that the right to have breakfast in public places ultimately derives from the right to assemble and demonstrate and the right of free expression of opinions.[1] One decidedly appealing effect of our efforts is that breakfast is politicised by taking it out of private contexts into the public sphere, but without losing its fun or sociable qualities.

Right of Assembly and a Culture of Permits

Independently of legal questions, the act of breakfasting in public is an outstanding tool to expand other ideas and models to the use of public spaces on principle. The common culture of permits – that is, the assumption that only that which is explicitly permitted is not forbidden – usually draws the laws of one's own possibilities far more narrowly than necessary and prematurely avoids real or imaginary conflicts. This restraint vis-à-vis modes of behaviour that are not explicit permitted and pre-formulated, vis-à-vis models that have not (yet) been established is deeply anchored in the culture. We ourselves still experience a little stage fright when we breakfast in especially prominent places. Even though, after years of experience to the contrary, we ought to know better, sometimes we still think that this time the police might show up, and we would have to debate with them, or they would try to drive us away. For that reason, it is inevitable that the practice of Permanent Breakfast cannot avoid developing and stipulating a new model for behaving in public, for example, the model of breakfasting in public. It is not about teaching passers-by proper, perhaps more courageous civic behaviour. Rather the point is to open up and encourage a palette of possibilities, so that new uses of public space that are adequate to the needs in question can be designed and implemented.

This naturally places demands on space and its qualities. From our point of view, what is needed is not installing permanent facilities for our use in streets, squares or in parks – say, tables and chairs for breakfasting. What results from the practice of breakfasting, from the search for appropriate locations, is the need for flexible spaces that do not predetermine a particular use but rather permit many different uses as the users desire. That – and about this we do not want there to be any doubt – is a political challenge, for what could be more political than the question of who has control over resources, especially public resources and public spaces.

1 The Austrian Constitutional Court classifies a meeting of several people to be an assembly within the meaning of the Law of Assembly (Versammlungsgesetz; VersG 1867; 1953) if it is organised with the intention of bringing those present to a shared activity (debate, discussion, demonstration, etc.), such that a certain association of the assembled results (Austrian Constitutional Court, collections 4586/63, 5193/66, 5195/66, 8685/79, 9783/83, 10443/85, 10 608/85, 10 955, 11 651/88, 11 866/88, 11 904/88, 11 935/88, 12 161/89). In other words, an assembly is a temporary formation of a number of people in a non-institutional community or a meeting of people (even in the street) for a common goal of discussing opinions or expressing opinions to others in order to produce a common action (cf. German Constitutional Court, 11.6.1991, EvR772/90, EUGRZ 1991, S 363); or collective expression of opinion with the objective of intellectual debate.

The Public Sphere and the Pseudo-Public Sphere

In practice, people breakfasting in Austria rarely push the limits of what the executive branch tolerates and must tolerate. Far more frequently, however, one does make the acquaintance of private security services when one sets up tables, chairs and a coffee pot in the relevant places.[2] The reason for that is the fact that public spaces and public institutions are increasingly being privatised. This development is by no means limited to Austria; indeed, one finds such privatisations in all European countries in the wake of neo-liberal developments. Permanent Breakfast is a project that makes the concrete effects of these policies visible and questions how these trends towards privatisation will effect the use of public spaces, indeed how they will effect the concept of the public sphere in general. There is, of course, no right to stay and assemble in private or privatised spaces as there is in public ones.

At this point it could be helpful to illustrate once again what qualities distinguish private and public spaces in general. In our experience, there are three very different kinds of spaces: private spaces, public spaces and pseudo-public spaces. Private spaces are, of course, those in which the owners set the rules: I decide who can enter my living room when I send out invitations to my garden party; and the owners of a company decide who can enter their store or factory. By contrast, public spaces are those in which the rules are determined by the public. In a democratic state, that is supposed to be the sovereign – namely, the people, or at least a

---

2 A breakfast in the museum district of Vienna was expelled from the courtyard of a large museum complex that is public property but is administered by a private operating company. Unwanted people and actions are also removed from the grounds of railway stations in Vienna belonging to the Österreichische Bundesbahn (ÖBB, Austrian Federal Railway), which has also been transformed into a private company.

representative of the people. One of the essential features of public spaces is, of course, free access to all, the right to spend time there. The right to assemble, demonstrate and express one's own views there are also granted. Permanent Breakfast tries to encourage everyone to use their collective property.

We referred to the third kind of space as pseudo-public. These are private spaces or spaces administrated by private companies that are disguised as public spaces, where a kind of pseudo-publicness is staged. Shopping centres are a good example, as many of them are organised in imitation of European city centres, equipped with street signs, indoor plazas, fountains and the like.

Even in Europe, such malls tend to be based on American models. One of the most prominent examples is the Forum Shops in Caesars Palace in Las Vegas: an establishment that has both the familiar attributes of urbanity, such as organisation on a pedestrian scale, a central marketplace and a structure copied from streetscapes. It is a special form of imitating public open spaces: a ceiling with painted clouds that is intended to simulate the course of the sun by changing the incidence of light. When the history is examined more closely, however, it turns out that the vocabulary of these malls was indeed taken from the context of European city centres. For example, Michael Zinganel has recently demonstrated convincingly, that the Jewish architect and urban planner Victor Gruen, who was exiled from Vienna, had Vienna in mind when planning the details of the organisation of his shopping centres.[3] *The mall*, which in the context of American cities 'serves as a substitute for the neglected public space of the inner cities',[4] is now migrating back to the edges of European cities, competing with its own precursor and even threatening its existence.

---

3 Michael Zinganel, 'Wien für Amerikaner', *dérive*, no. 3 (February 2001), pp. 4–6.
4 Ibid., p. 4.

The images of publicness that are evoked in shopping centres are clearly attractive and are used to draw in customers. These images can certainly obscure the fact that many essential aspects of publicness are lacking here, above all the simple right to stay in these spaces. Strictly speaking the private owners or operators do not even have to give a reason for expelling unwanted visitors from these locations. In these pseudo-public spaces, demonstrations are not permitted; homeless people cannot stay here and of course there is no right to assemble to exchange opinions freely. As long as one wants to shop, has a bank card and, in some cases, does not have an unwelcome skin colour, these limitations pose no problem. But apparently even the paying customers of the large shopping centres do not wish to be reduced to the role of pure consumers, so that one has to offer them an urban ambiance and at least a few signs of public space.

Another kind of pseudo-public space is the privatisation of formerly public institutions. The transformation of once public spaces like museums, railway stations and parks seems more problematic to us than the existence of shopping centres. One is used to thinking of them as public spaces and, if no occasion arises, one scarcely notices that they no longer are. For in the name of budget cutting or even tax savings, countless former public institutions have been sold or transformed into private companies in recent years. Gradually, an ideological reorientation is taking place that questions the concept of the public sphere per se. As formerly public spaces are stripped of universal access and use, and hence of their public character, it corroborates a point of view that wants to see state institutions reduced to the administration of private interests.

In contrast to that view, we think that the public sphere is more, and should be more, than the sum of private interests. The difference between the two viewpoints on how to approach public space can be clarified concretely: rights such as the right to use a space, the right to assemble, to debate, to demonstrate and to express one's own opinion are directly tied to the existence of public spaces. Private spaces are, however they may be designed, no substitute for that.

Disguising private, commercial spaces as public ones and the transformation of public locations into privately managed ones is making it increasingly difficult to tell what kind of space one is located in. Permanent Breakfast is a very handy litmus test to ensure oneself that a space is public. For breakfasting in public always means insisting on the right to assembly, to speak publicly and to use public resources. Any place one can have breakfast is therefore a public space, and vice versa: a space, or at least a free space, where one cannot have breakfast is not a real public space. The place and time of an assembly create a direct, socio-political field of tension between legislation regarding the use of public space and those using it. A breakfast in a public space should, therefore, always be seen as a political act as well.

Sovereignty

Fortunately, despite government austerity measures and a reorganisation of public institutions based on neo-conservative motives, there is still plenty of public space where one can have breakfast: streets, squares, parks, traffic islands, parking lots and so on.

Naturally, the beautiful locations, the successful plazas and especially the former spaces of the nobility should be used. Every year on 1 May we have breakfast on Heldenplatz in Vienna, in the former front garden of the imperial castle. An everyday action like having breakfast on the Hofburg grounds also plays with the image of the sovereign, who was once an emperor, and who could use the castle's extensive grounds to satisfy his private needs. In a democratic context, being sovereign could also mean appropriating the sensory pleasure of these spaces on a daily basis. Palace gardens for everyone, not just to be seen and photographed by tourists, but to be lived in. If one leaves the Vienna castle and heads to the old and new suburbs, it often becomes more restricted. It is not always the result of a lack of space. We refer to one phenomenon we often encounter as *horror vacui,* the fear of the empty place. One could almost formulate it as a rule: everywhere where space is particularly limited, you can be sure something will be standing in the way: a flowerbox, a bed of tulips, a bench, a fountain, some piece of art. In the middle of the plaza, as a rule. Perhaps these things were placed there to provide sensory pleasure for the sovereign, so that he didn't have to go to the Hofburg or to a museum every time he felt the need to see something beautiful. But perhaps these things are also there so that no one gets the idea that the plaza could be used. The sovereign, who on every halfway decent spring day seeks out in droves his former hunting grounds in Vienna's Prater park, to smell the grass, skate, play ball, play music or to picnic, might otherwise get the idea to do the same thing here. But perhaps it is also the case that very many of these people who spend their existences planning and beautifying such places suffer from a variety of *horror vacui* that prevents them from letting the object of their design be empty. Nothing is better suited to overcoming this fear than a full, well-placed breakfast table.

Vacancies and Urban Reserves

As utopias develop more and more into 'forbidden places', the desire loses its potential and the terrain lacks creators. As a result, the desire more frequently becomes prefabricated and compulsive. The wishes addressing a city have become particularly interchangeable and stale. As early as the year 2000, at *deseo urbano* in Valparaíso, Chile, transparadiso made the potential of wishing a major theme of an urban intervention.[1] It was already clear at the time that urbanists should also become 'wish consultants', just as architects can often work out what their private clients desire in meetings that resemble therapy sessions. Maintaining vacancies as 'released spaces/liberated spaces' (or spaces of desires) means providing space for the unknown wish and thus creating desire – desire to have a say in development and allow oneself to be led by the fiction that one can really have influence. In the project *wishing released* recently realised in Salzburg, transparadiso played the role of 'wish consultants'. The project was a contribution to Trichtlinnburg, a European Union project involving the cities of Maastricht, Salzburg and Tallinn, which was, not least, about the relationship between tourism and vacancy.[2] For situations like these that call for direct action in urban space, because conventional planning approaches have long since been cancelled out by pure market forces, transparadiso has been developing the Indikatormobil since 2002 – an urban vehicle as a flexible tool for 'direct

transparadiso

Barbara Holub,
Paul Rajakovics

1 Using a puzzle-like board game, the residents' wishes were presented to the city, using wish cards that were divided into new urban-development categories like *salmón* (salmon), *adelante* (forwards), *aparición/apariencia* (apparition).

urbanism'. For Trichtlinnburg, the Indikatormobil served as a temporary, mobile programme generator and central location for 'wish consultants' who promoted the voluntary refusal to keep shops vacant, as a potential for the spontaneous development of wishes for the specific location (in this case, empty shops or buildings).[3]

Until recently 'releasing' (spaces) could not yet be much more than a perspective for sites that were neither occupied nor planned, and the Indikatormobil as a new tool for tactical and 'ambulant' urbanism was still in the 'immaterial' phase of development as a research project. Nevertheless, thanks to the realisation of several projects with the Indikatormobil, the elements of the Indikatormobil as a tool/instrument and the method of 'releasing' as an urbanistic task, both existing parallel, have truly solidified into a common evolution. The wish that it would be possible to accomplish the goal of developing new programmes by employing our special instrument was confirmed. Our interest in the EU project was in initiating a process that dared to take risks in wishing beyond any 'feasibility', rather than leading to short-term consumption of culture. Out of the difference between the concrete wish and the unknown, a potential can develop that cannot be imagined in detail yet. This uncertainty, which can be produced, for example, by temporary 'releasing', contradicts the usual logic of planning and for that reason needs other sets of instruments and other actors. Park Fiction in Hamburg is an outstanding post-1968 urbanistic project – an example for such a practice, in which a col-

2 Salzburg played a special role in this: in contrast to the other two cities, Salzburg's old town has scarcely any vacant space at all. Because lease and purchase prices in Salzburg are very high, there are few opportunities for newcomers or intellectuals to develop a diverse scene independent of tourist-orientated uses. Salzburg's chance for psycho-geographic regeneration is thus extremely limited. The few available spaces evade a non-economic approach.

lective insistence on a wish put a stop to an investment project that would have affected the district. Park Fiction managed to develop an alternative project with no short-term economic potential (a park) that succeeded in replacing a project based on real-estate speculation. The discursive success of this project ultimately lies in the combination of a collective wish, which is expressed in the rejection of neo-liberal economic thinking and wants in principle to keep an area open, and the resistance that still clings to the hope that it can assert itself against an authority.

3 Together with Initiative Architektur and several owners of empty business in the left side of the old town, we developed an intervention that suggested the potential vacancies have (rather than stigmatising them) and removed them from economic exploitation. In the end, it did not matter why a given building stood empty. We designed posters which were mounted like wallpapers covering up the windows of the vacancies and creating new 'façades' for a future function. Vacancies were thus marked as the city's reserves and turned into projection screens for the desires of the participants in the project. At the Indikatormobil, 'wish consultants' were on the spot as urbanistic guides, helping to generate wishes beyond economical constraints of high lease rates. They distributed keys to the empty shops which were marked on a special map to be discovered by the project participants in an unusual way. Since only some of the keys fit, 'spies' waited around the other shops to open them on demand. A video was produced especially to be shown on the Indikatormobil, advertising the vacant units with the whispering voice of personal and collective desires. These 'topographies of desire', which were also broadcast on the radio as invitations to participate, were: the anti-grumbling bar, a chill-out, narrated spaces, vertical plantations on Steingasse, sunlight in the basement, a rain-free zone, a clubhouse for losers, a scream room, a revolution centre, a school for smelling, a steam bath, a Hindu temple, a free zone for lesbians and gays, the treasure chamber, a lilac salon, the million decibel pub, the training centre for safecrackers, a free space, space for reserves....

Wishing released, Salzburg 2005
Movie screening in 'Indikatormobil'
deseo urbano, urban intervention with a game, Valparaiso 2001

Wishing released, Salzburg 2005
Freed shop
Wish consulting

117

At precisely this point a sensitive field in urbanism opens up that can redefine urban development between tactical intervention and strategic thinking. One could call the space between the two the 'poetic reserve', another kind of 'investment in the future', whose programmes can only be determined via a time hole that creates space for the unknown. Liberating spaces ('releasing')[4] provides the breathing room a city needs. Simply by wishing for it, this reserve can be activated and thus freed from its previous context, just as an image can be extracted from its background or cropped in the graphic programme Photoshop and thus prepared for a new context. This, of course, also opens up the abyss for price speculation and encourages omissions. It is easy to open up as a reserve a property with little potential value. But liberating spaces means saving what is perhaps the most valuable part. The urban reserve must be independent of the possibility of financial exploitation, which also means that there can be no pressure to exploit. 'Releasing' consciously resists this economic pressure in order to create a still greater collective value over the long term. Into the 1980s, the communes attempted – in the spirit of classical urban planning – to take over this task. In the meanwhile, however, even public properties have long since begun to be exploited by the private sector, which makes it much more difficult to remove properties from monetary considerations. 'Releasing' is based on an expanded notion of capital that, in the spirit of Pierre Bourdieu,

4 The use of the German verb *freistellen* is a reference to the meaning it has in the graphic programme Photoshop (to crop or extract an image from its background), but is here introduced as an urbanistic strategy in the sense of releasing, liberating spaces from their original or market orientated uses. *Freistellen* would literally mean 'to free spaces' and alludes to the possibility of an extracted image serving as space of projection – for new wishes. *Freistellen* is thus translated in its various meanings as *releasing spaces, liberating spaces* and *vacancies*.

considers cultural and social capital to be of at least equal value to financial capital. 'Releasing' works with the non-assessable, unknown desire and with the invaluable. A new potential evolves out of the difference between concrete desire and the unknown. Traditional urban development, by contrast, is defined by the tangible, the imagined goal. Borrowing from physics, a kind of 'uncertainty principle' helps to clarify questions of urban development. Because the future per se cannot be defined, but is rather comparable to an equation with an infinite number of variables, the uncertainty principle only functions where it is essential in the imagination. The vague fiction is thus more likely to generate the future than a fixed idea. The frustration that a precise idea has not been formed is substituted by the possible. 'Releasing' thus means remaining open to desires and fictions that should not be fulfilled immediately. These desires oscillate between private and collective ideas that have to be first channelled and focused. This opens up a new field of tasks for urbanists that means mediating between the personal drive for conquest, self-censorship and collective needs as well as the usual professional parameters. The question then is how methods like those of Park Fiction, which were based on a private initiative of artists, can be applied to urbanism, but without instrumentalising or disabling the sometimes oppositional methods that operate by means of unexpected turns. 'Releasing', however, is surely a luxury that our society can afford.

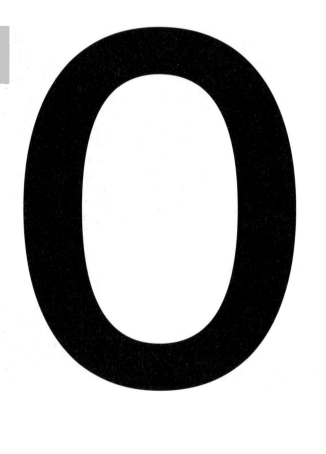

projects

Title	Radioballett
Type	an interventionist way of listening to the radio
Type of use	cultural

Location	many different public places, for example, a pedestrian precinct in Munich
Time	since 2002, for example, 9 February 2005
	less than one hour each

Initiators	LIGNA (Ole Frahm, Michael Hueners, Torsten Michaelsen), radio builders
Temporary users	interventionist radio listeners
Role of city	none
Status	legal

Goals	LIGNA tries to change listeners to a temporary association through different models of radio use. This association can infiltrate the laws and standards of different public and private spaces and lay claim to its own space. Listening to the radio becomes intervention – and a practice of change.

www.radioballett.tk

radioballett

The independent radio group LIGNA develops concepts that enable radio to intervene in controlled public spaces in such a way that their publicness appears to be an uncontrollable situation. If counter-publicness is essentially based on broadcasting the correct contents in traditional formats, Radioballett is concerned with intervening in public spaces and of thus creating a 'new format' – that of interventionist radio listening. If the concept of counter-publicness is concerned with listeners' development of political effectiveness outside the radio transmission, the concept of interventionist publicness is about allowing listening to the radio to become effective in itself. A Radioballett is not a gathering, but instead a dispersion. It has no consistent stage. It takes no particular shape and exists only in a concurrent, and yet dispersed gesture. It does not hinder passers-by, but instead irritates through its simultaneousness. No particular talent as a dancer is necessary to take part in this ballet. One only needs to have an attentive ear and a portable radio with earphones. Roughly distributed throughout a pedestrian precinct, participants, by listening to the radio, are instructed to carry out certain activities. The Radioballett can be received everywhere in the vicinity, just like any other radio programme, but is intended for a specific location. A Radioballett took place in Munich in 2005. As a prelude to protests against the NATO Security Conference approximately 300 radio ballet-dancers attended. The Munich Radioballett was broadcast by Radio Lora 92.4 and allowed people to dance for nearly a half an hour. They begged passers-by, stuck to the shop-windows at the temples of consumption, ran screaming or jumping through the crowd and moved at times in a serious fashion, at times in an amusing fashion through the pedestrian precinct. Because observers were confused at first, flyers were handed out to make the event more accessible to them.

Title	Spaziergangswissenschaft
Type	walking as the smallest possible form of planning intervention
Type of use	planning

Location	many different locations, including Dönche, Kassel; Bovisa, Milan
Time	since the 1980s
	two hours

Initiator	Lucius Burckhardt, planning theoretician
Temporary users	walkers
Role of city	none
Status	legal

Goals The Burckhardtian 'basic understanding of the complex system of social environments was developed as an attempt to bring planning closer to the everyday world. The vagueness and unpredictability of the development and state of urban systems confronts planning to an ever greater extent with the inadequacy of its own instruments. To clearly recognise this and to research methods of investigating the reality and the dynamism of possible intervention is an urgent task at the present time.' (Jesko Fezer and Martin Schmitz, 'Lucius Burckhardt, "Wer plant die Planung?"' in Klaus Selle, *Planung neu denken*, Dortmund, 2006).

www.lucius-burckhardt.org; Lucius Burckhardt, *Warum ist Landschaft schön? Die Spaziergangswissenschaft*, Berlin, 2006.

spaziergangswissenschaft

Lucius Burckhardt founded a new science in the 1980s: Spaziergangswissenschaft (Walking Science), also known as Promenadology or Strollology. An intellectual force in the criticism of urbanism – he has dealt with planning and building in a democracy since the early 1950s – he has gathered his research together with the use of this concept. *The Journey to Tahiti,* which began with a trip to the Dönche, a former military training ground near Kassel, is Walking Science's most important artistic manifestation and was organised together with students. This trip was repeated in 1988 at the 17th Triennial in Milan – at the Bovisa, a strange mixture of industrial wasteland and brightly coloured southern flora, unused tracks with remnants of the railroad, the *cascine* (farmhouses) and noble villas. The journey was modelled on that of Captain Cook and Georg Forster, who went to Tahiti in 1772. Those who travelled to Kassel and Milan, however, went by bus or train: They moved in a big loop through the respective areas and heard extracts from Forster's diary at ten different locations. They heard about Tahiti while viewing the Dönche or Bovisa. Burckhardt wrote in his travel programme: What do discoverers discover? This question originated from a seminar where various texts were read about landscapes. Poets and travellers wrote about those areas they had visited – but what did they actually see there? And did they convey to the reader that which is really special there, or only the standard repertoire of landscape descriptions found in the literary genre: charming meadows, steep gorges, distant mountains? And if the concept of landscape is already defined in this way in literature, what do discoverers really see? But perhaps that what is new is also at home here, the students in Kassel asked themselves, and decided to research Forster's text about Tahiti in an area near Kassel. Perhaps the descriptions of this heavenly island apply to an abandoned military training ground?

Falt-Plan
für die Fahrt nach Tahiti

Abfahrt der Segelschiffe:
Donnerstag, den 18. Juni 1987,
14 Uhr in Kassel am Holländischen Platz
Henschelstraße 2

Dauer ca. 3 Stunden. Gute Schuhe, Ruck-
sack und Badehose sind mitzubringen.

Sprecher:
Peter Lüchinger, Staatstheater Kassel

Fahrkarte incl. Fliegenklatsche 5 DM

Vorverkauf: K10, Raum 302

Auswärtige Teilnehmer bitten wir um
Anmeldung bei:
Gesamthochschule Kassel GhK, Fach-
bereich Stadtplanung/Landschaftsplanung -
FB 13, Henschelstraße 2, D 3500 Kassel

Verantwortlich i.S.d.P. Lucius Burckhardt

Title	Circle Line Party
Type	temporary use of an underground train as a party room
Type of use	entertainment
Location	trains of the London Underground, Circle Line
Time	for the first time in March 1999, several times since then; the party described took place in 2003 several hours
Initiators	Space Hijackers, in existence since 1999
Temporary users	party guests
Role of city	none
Status	semi-legal
Goals	The idea behind the party was an expression of freedom and protest against the repressive, war-like politics of greedy white men who want to rule the world – an attempt to promote do-it-yourself culture in an age of unrestrained consumerism, to create a place for human interaction which is far from the clutches of capitalism and finally, to play a nasty trick on those who destroy civil rights and non-commercialised fun.

www.spacehijackers.org

circle line party

The Circle Line Party is a celebration on the Circle Line, a circuitous London underground line. A planning group was put together a few weeks before the date of the party and a website started with tips about how to do a round, have fun and not have any problems. Careful planning concerning how people and equipment could be smuggled onto the train was necessary. A stereo system, bar and podium for pole dancing had to be camouflaged as normal luggage. In order to remain undiscovered for the longest possible time the party should only take place in tunnels – in the stations everything remained quiet, at least as long as no one was drunk. People were supposed to bring costumes with them that could be changed into and out of quickly so that within an instant they could change from being commuters in suits to party animals and back. When everything was ready there were about 600 party-goers at the arranged meeting point. Initial access was at the Liverpool Street Station, one of the few stations big enough to smuggle so many people in without becoming suspicious. The guard at the platform attempted to get everyone to spread out along its entire length, while the party-goers wanted to stay as far back as possible so that the driver wouldn't hear any music. The party crowd filled four complete carriages. It took a few stations after departing before the music system was set up. A samba band played in the last carriage, the DJ installed loudspeakers in the second and third carriage and played music to fit the occasion, the pole dancers danced and alcohol flowed like water. The trains were decorated: colour transparencies were placed in front of the lights, mirrored balls hung on the railings and a lot of balloons were used. After a time the party got too loud and all of a sudden, during the second trip round, the British Transport Police arrived on the scene. Instead of throwing all the party-goers off the train, the trip was instead ended at Moorgate Station. Some stayed behind in order to straighten things up.

Title Permanent Breakfast
Type private use of public space as a test of just how public it is
Type of use gastronomical

Location public space,
chosen by those having breakfast
Time since 1 May 1996, with no end in sight
several hours each time

Initiator Friedemann Derschmidt, artist
Temporary users approximately 300 breakfasts are listed on the website, with
ten participants per breakfast this adds up to 3,000 people –
in addition there is a large number of unknown breakfasts.
Role of city none
Status legal

Goals Permanent Breakfast is a game, an art project, art in public
spaces and public art, but also urban planning, a social
project or a tool for investigating the quality of public space
or for insuring the public character of a particular space.

www.permanentbreakfast.org

permanent breakfast

On the morning of the 1 May 1996 a group of artists began to have breakfast in a public space, namely at Vienna's Schwarzenbergplatz, a symbolically highly charged location which now serves as a traffic intersection. The basic idea is simple but attractive: a person invites guests to a public breakfast – and each one of those invited is obliged to organise a similar breakfast at another location with other participants, etc. According to the snowball principle, if four guests were invited to each breakfast every day for ten days there would be a total of 1.4 million people taking part in a public breakfast. This principle was given the name Permanent Breakfast, 'rules of the game' were drawn up and published, and over the years the public breakfast became a cult. Hundreds have been documented over the years in places like Berlin, Prague, Oslo, New York, Jerusalem and Melbourne. The snowball principle, the intention of which was to bring a large number of people eating breakfast into the street, no longer plays a central role, but instead the question of accessibility of public space and the illustration of spatial situations which require increased attention. This is expressed by the fact that breakfasts have taken place along the borders between the Czech Republic, Slovakia, Hungary and Austria. Those participating in such a breakfast change the public space they are in: they become their own medium of spatial occupation and spatial change – again and again. It is possible to precisely gauge the understanding of just how public a location is by observing the reactions of other users and 'protectors' of the public space. The Permanent Breakfast thus becomes a sort of litmus test for the accessibility of public space. In carrying out such breakfasts, it is possible to reveal the superficial look of invisible spatial situations, such as private, formerly public spaces or publicly disguised private spaces.

Title	Reclaim the Streets!
Type	temporary use of streets for unregistered parties and protests
Type of use	political, cultural
Location	London and many other cities worldwide
Time	since the mid-1990s in each case a few hours
Initiator	Reclaim the Streets! is not an organisation, but a network
Temporary users	several hundred to tens of thousands of street users
Role of city	none
Status	illegal
Goals	use of public space for parties and the simultaneous denial of this space for the otherwise privileged traffic and consumer usage

rts.gn.apc.org

reclaim the streets!

The concept of Reclaim the Streets! is simple: For a short time public space should be taken over, namely with the help of a large number of bodies, with creativity and music. In doing so, to make police interference less probable, it has to be friendlier than conventional political demonstrations but at the same time cause enough disturbance to the daily routine of traffic and consumers. The concept originated in London in the mid-1990s and was mainly concerned with the criticism of automobile traffic. It all started with numerous occupations of construction sites belonging to a large road construction programme in the early 1990s, which began with the occupation of a building site at an access ramp for the M11 motorway (since opened) which went through a residential area in London, reaching the city in 1993 and brushing ecological and social concerns aside. Daily vehicular traffic forms one of the foundations of London's economy, as in every European city, which is why the negative consequences are barely given any attention. Against this background it was possible to make the concerns of the unregistered street parties plausible to the middle-class press and hence to a broader public in general. The various party locations spread out at short notice via telephone or by word of mouth, just like with raves. The Criminal Justice Act was introduced in 1994 to deal with this and other new kinds of civil disobedience, and allowed for the breaking up of parties, thus becoming a point of attack for Reclaim the Streets! Reclaim the Streets! wants to open up the street, which is common property but now designated as 'enclosed', to the public at large by denying it to drivers. It is therefore not just ecological concerns which matter, but criticism of capitalism as well. At the latest since the global action day on 16 May 1998 the Reclaim the Streets! principle has been copied around the world, especially in European, American and Australian cities.

Title Urban Cabaret
Type mobile exhibits concerning urban development, discussion groups
Type of use social, planning

Location numerous locations in Glasgow, Scotland, among others
Pollokshaws, Dennistoun, Parkhead, Merchant City, North
Kelvinside, Govanhill, Partick, Kelvingrove, Possil, Gorbals,
Cowcaddens, Townhead, Kingston, Breahead, Scotstoun,
Calton, Blythwood, Finnieston, Woodlands, Gernethill,
Strathbungo, Crosshill, Shawlands, Priesthill, Anderston,
Pollokshields, Hyndland

Time 14–29 September 2001
several hours each time during a two-week time period

Initiator Glas (Glasgow Letters on Architecture and Space)
Temporary users local residents
Role of city none
Status legal

Goals making questions about urban development an issue in
local communities

www.glas-collective.com

urban cabaret

Glas has existed since 2000 and is a cooperative of thirteen architects, teachers, authors and urban activists which carries out projects for local communities in Glasgow. Glas examines the causes and effects of unequal development within our built environment. They are concerned with privatisation, miserable living conditions, uninspired institutions and closed swimming pools just as much as shopping centres, motorways and security firms. By producing critical multimedia projects Glas attempts to provoke a political change of view concerning the way we shape and perceive our cities, and where possible to change the prevailing policy of capitalistic production and the use of the built environment. Urban Cabaret comprises a series of events in Glasgow. Among them were mobile exhibitions as well as discussions with groups which were involved in arguments concerning changes in their environment. In addition the magazine *glaspaper* was distributed. Specific contradictions and injustices in today's European cities were to be discussed, such as the privatisation of space, public surveillance, the tyranny of trade, the manifestation of gender, race and class-specific discrimination, ownership and control of the city itself, and the means with which these are produced. For this purpose a bright red Piaggio Ape, a three-wheeled transporter, was used to carry elements of the exhibition contained in record boxes. The Ape, which carried a labelled structure that shone at night, was parked at strategic locations, such as intersections, an entrance to a shopping mall or at a small plaza, in the outskirts of the city as well as in the downtown area. The basic principle was to go to the people instead of wanting to bring them to an institution, thus creating networks between experts and affected persons.

Title	kein Geld
Type	party platform for people with no money
Type of use	cultural

Location	six locations in the Viennese Prater
Time	end of July until end of August 2004
	six times, in each case for an evening

Initiators	Susanne Schuda, Florian Schmeiser, Peter Koger, artists
Temporary users	users of the equipment, party guests
Role of city	none
Status	semi-legal

Goals The project reflects the production of values and their conditions in general. It asks a question about the psychological, social and political meaning of kein Geld (no money), of self-esteem, social nets due to personal relationships, and the visibility of money, and offers the opportunity to experimentally revalue these symbols by participating in a social sculpture.

www.keingeld.at

kein geld

The project's theme dealt with the strategies of people, most of whom were active in the context of art, who had no money but wanted nevertheless to play a role. As part of the kein Geld project, participants were urged to avoid consumption and to instead become involved and be creative. The motto was 'No one gets anything for free'. For this purpose equipment was placed at their disposal on six summer evenings in different locations within the Viennese Prater recreational area, the use of which was to enable them to be creative. This equipment consisted of a 'mobile', a handcart which served as the basis for a series of 'connective possibilities': a music system powered by an electrical generator, a hotplate with cooking and eating utensils and a refrigerator, complete with lighting and blankets for comfortable picnicking. This was the equipment provided for a stay in the park, which didn't cost anything and offered many possibilities of being self-sufficient. The social experiment consisted of people with monetary problems and their strategies of dealing with this, of the relationship between them, their actions and non-actions on site. Every evening there were musicians and cooks who 'played' with the infrastructure, thus providing an interesting framework for the others, who were urged, however, not simply to come, but to bring joyfulness, music and food with them. In this way value was increased, even if there was 'no money'. Social contact or a lack thereof, restrictions and exclusion from segments of society are the result of monetary problems. This occurs at spatial, structural and interpersonal levels. Kein Geld experiments with forms of self-support and external help on the basis of a voluntary exchange, of symbiotic relationships where the boundaries between providers and those provided for, the service sector and consumers, and supply and demand are either continuously defined anew or dissolved.

Title instant island
Type temporary art space in a peripheral context
Type of use cultural

Location empty business premises in the Wien-Nord train station
Time July to September 1999 and once for 48 hours during
the summer of 2000
for one evening each time

Initiators Susanne Schuda, Florian Schmeiser, Nik Hummer, artists
Temporary users musicians, guests
Role of city sponsor
Status legal

Goals Exemplary investigation of the meaning of living and life in
the city, of how ways of life are determined, of which
behavioural patterns are possible in public space and in the
so-called private sphere, using as an example the peripheral
Wien-Nord train station.

instant island

A business premises in the elevated Wien-Nord train station with a direct view of the Praterstern motorway roundabout. The train station was built in the 1950s and has remained unchanged since. instant island was implanted into this location. Passers-by seldom went past – sometimes tourists got lost here while searching for the Ferris wheel. Other local users, travellers, commuters, the homeless, shoppers and recreation-seekers hadn't used the deserted automobile tunnel for a long time. The Praterstern, with its clear separation of individual and public traffic, formed an anonymous backdrop. The planned functionalism of the traffic area corresponded to the functionalisation of ways of life, the restriction of individual behaviour. Those who had crossed this boundary and therefore no longer belonged anywhere were assembled here and were also a reason for the neglect of the place. Two bunk beds with monitors were installed in the store; they were similar to cubicles found in capsule hotels in Tokyo. All surfaces were covered with plastic and the only points of 'attack' were an access ladder, the capsule itself and the capsule lid, which was closed upon entering in order to escape the exposure contained within the anonymity in the capsule's intimacy. Inside there was enough room to lie down and watch the programme on the monitor. The television was necessary in order to provide the tight space with a window to the outside. The implantation, as an artificial foreign element, set itself apart from the peripheral Praterstern area which made two things visible: the site's specificity and its relationship with the very different object that was instant island, an island in the stream. It remains unclear what instant island actually was: architecture, an installation, a concert, a video programme, a field study or an offer for consumers of the urban scene on the periphery.

Title	kraut
Type	mobile newspaper
Type of use	cultural

Location	twenty different locations in Germany
Time	May until November 2004
	over a period of five months, for one day each time

Initiators	Christian Lagé, artist
Temporary users	twenty editors in rotation (four times) and passers-by
Role of city	none
Status	legal

Goals the old system has been discarded and we are on our way to a new world. But what will it look like? Phrases like 'deal with it', 'stick it out', 'willingness to make sacrifices' and 'be reasonable' are making the rounds. Times are tough and we are taking them seriously. Is there actually such a lack of fantasy, is it so trite: those on the top and the rest of us down here, and in between a diffuse and religious-sounding concept of an economic boom which just doesn't want to fly? There is a lack of communication in Germany and in the middle of this commotion a lot of people who have something to say. This is exactly where kraut comes in and collects the views, voices and moods of people who live in Germany.

www.anschlaege.de/kraut

kraut

kraut was a newsstand, a newspaper with a small editorial office, a mobile speaker's corner on a trip through Germany. kraut was underway for five months and published newspapers at twenty different locations, for a week each time. The central themes were locally volatile issues, matters of minor importance, observations made on site, collected views, voices and moods as well as everything the local population requested to have published. The contents were therefore not only put together by the editorial staff, but were also contributed by local residents. Every love letter was published as was a world conspiracy theory and a draft of a new constitution. The quality of kraut was dependent on the editors. The goal was not to find the most experienced journalists, but creative people instead. This interdisciplinary editorial team changed every month. The weekly order of events involved moving to a new location on Monday, getting orientated, making contact and collecting weekly subject matter on Tuesday and producing one issue per day (there were thus four issues per location and week) from Wednesday to Saturday. Sundays were off. A new topic of interest was decided upon every morning. Contents were then gathered and put together in a layout during the evening. The results of the day were then duplicated without delay on a copier: 200 copies, A3, black and white, folded and cut. A discarded and converted kiosk from the Berlin sanitation department served as the kraut kiosk. In the smallest possible space there was room not only for the equipment necessary for daily newspaper work, but for possibilities before, in between and afterwards as well. At the end of a week, after the work was done, the kraut kiosk was loaded onto a transporter and driven to the next location.

kraut №00043

kraut №00057

krant №00065

kraut №00069

kraut №00034

kraut №00024

kraut

157

Title Camp for Oppositional Architecture
Type convention, temporary hotel and venue
Type of use political, cultural

Location empty factory in Berlin-Wedding
Time June 2004
three days

Initiators *An Architektur,* architecture magazine
Temporary users conference participants
Role of city none
Status legal

Goals The conference attempted to put an 'architecture of reality'
on the agenda, to address the subject of a segregated
and thoroughly economised world.

www.anarchitektur.com

oppositional architecture

The magazine *An Architektur* was founded in 2002 by the urban-political architecture collective freies fach, a group which, through diverse activities, exhibitions and short publications, chose the then restrictive Berlin urban restructuring and its political and economic background as a central theme. The theme of the congress organised by *An Architektur* was an increasing dissatisfaction among young planners with the globalised culture of commodified spaces, for which classical architecture and its theory no longer have answers. Critical architecture has to have an understanding of its own general conditions and take part in the struggle for a better world. Questions had to be asked as to which progressive social role architects could take upon themselves, which possibilities of action were there in planning, whether possibilities within the field of planning exist to challenge the current social order, and what the relevant practices and strategies of opposition could be. The Camp for Oppositional Architecture in Berlin was an open convention with approximately 100 participants from more than 16 countries who discussed a critical positioning. Three workshops concerning the subjects of oppositional social engagement, oppositional design strategies and oppositional strategies of intervention were formed. The convention's end result was a Preliminary Charter of Oppositional Architecture, which was intended to serve as a reference for future detailed discussions. In spite of the relatively low number of people at the conference an intensive global network was created among participants, which has continued to function until today. Anyone who had a pertinent contribution to make was welcome to participate, and was given a place to sleep in the factory and provided with food during the convention. Necessary furnishing in the empty halls was created simply by means of reusable plastic crates and second-hand furniture.

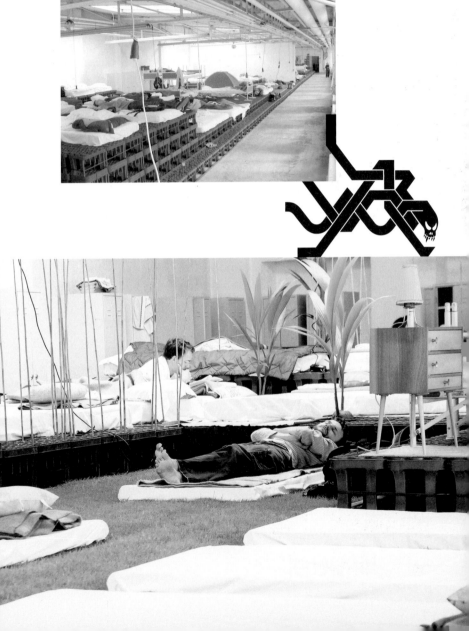

Title	Hirnsegel #7
Type	experiment concerning programme development
Type of use	cultural

Location	last of all at Südtirolerplatz, before that at six locations in Vienna: Kunsthalle Karlsplatz, Ramperstorffergasse, Retentionsbecken Auhof, Eisvogelgasse, Wehr Donaukanal, Garage Westbahnhof
Time	seven times between 1992 and 1995 in each case from several days to a week

Initiators	Florian Haydn, Marie-Therese Harnoncourt, Ernst J. Fuchs the POOR BOYs ENTERPRISE
Temporary users	approximately 700 visitors in all
Role of city	none
Status	legal

Goals	The general public's attention should be drawn to the potential of unused space in the city

hirnsegel

Over the course of several years the concrete columns under the railway bridge were completely covered by advertising posters and announcements of future events in the city. Using a technique similar to that of fixing posters, columns for Hirnsegel #7 (Brainsail #7) were wrapped in a plastic membrane so that they created a room between the columns. This newly created room was an empty space and offered new possibilities. In contrast to the sought-after locations everywhere in the city, there was no programme whatsoever for these sites. The membrane, a poster in itself which referred to the space it created, was available for any possible programmes and uses which occurred during the existence of this empty space. Getting the 'brain to sail' was the starting point for the space that was created here. The users were discoverers, it was intended to encourage the discovery of uses, and preconceived definitions and functional division were to be left behind. As the Hirnsegel idea was being developed, suitable locations in Vienna were searched for and marked. The location of Hirnsegel #7 was under the Südbahn underpass, a bottleneck between the city's inner and southern districts, traffic-wise one of the most densely used places. The Südbahn motorway, underground, streetcars, rapid-transit railroad, cars and pedestrians all cross paths here. Each area between the bridge's supporting columns was originally taken up by some kind of traffic flow. As a result of a reorganisation of traffic, one single section between the columns was no longer used. This 'emptiness' was to be opened up and extended for discoverers. The tightly stretched tarpaulin, 89 metres long and four metres high, formed a 330 m² large space, which was urban in character and had no function. The space was made available for seven days. The collection of sites marked with 'brain-sails' was an arrangement of personal mental projection areas which pointed to the potential of emptiness and dysfunctionalism.

Title Traumkombinat
Type art project in an empty department store
Type of use cultural

Location Hohenstücken, Brandenburg, Germany
Time July 2004
one week

Initiator Florian Gass, Club Real, artist
Temporary users residents, children, visitors from Berlin
Role of city sponsor
Status legal, lack of building permit tolerated

Goals As part of the varied efforts of Brandenburg's communities to find strategies for the problems of shrinking urban regions, the intention was to give an impulse to the idea that the identity of a neighbourhood is not based on the aim of economic development alone.

Information: www.clubreal.de

traumkombinat

The Traumkombinat (Dream Collective) was an unusual place to spend the night, and helped visitors focus their attention on their own dreams, inspired through the antique practice of incubation (sleep in the sanctum of a god or hero). To that end, an empty GDR department store, which had never been opened, was furnished as a dormitory where people had the opportunity to spend one night devoting themselves exclusively to dreaming. The design of the space as a dream collective included an area for preparation and a lounge as well as an inner sleeping area, the centre of which contained a dream catalyst. The staging of the advent and opening of the catalyst as part of a procession of escape from the Brandenburg train station to the collective in a neighbourhood consisting of prefabricated concrete tower blocks drew the local population's attention to the use of the so-called 'investment ruins'. Ten to twenty people visited the collective each night. After an introduction to the practice of dream cartography, guests were led to their sleeping quarters surrounding the dream catalyst. Here they viewed the play *Contestants* before falling asleep. After spending a maximum of eight hours dreaming, guests were awakened so they could record their dreams. A common breakfast in front of the collective made up the final part of the dreaming experience. In addition to visitors from Berlin, Potsdam and Leipzig, children and young people from the surrounding area were inspired to use the dream collective. Occasional disturbances at night by rowdies were dealt with by working with the Brandenburger Jugendkulturfabrik (Youth culture factory) and by expanding the programme to include quiet and nightmare-nights, thus contributing to public exposure for the project.

SCHLAF-SAAL

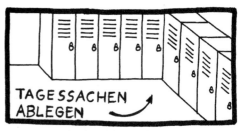

TAGESSACHEN
ABLEGEN

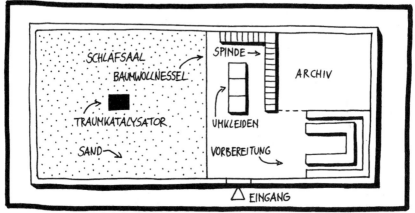

SCHLAFSAAL
BAUMWOLLNESSEL
SPINDE →

ARCHIV

TRAUMKATALYSATOR

UMKLEIDEN

SAND →

VORBEREITUNG

△ EINGANG

Title	Cabin Exchange
Type	temporary rooms for artists and communities
Type of use	artistic
Location	various locations in Glasgow and Edinburgh
Time	since 2002, repeated annually in each case for one week
Initiator	Will Foster, artist
Temporary users	all passers-by
Role of city	none
Status	legal
Goals	offering inexpensive and accessible public exhibition space for artists

www.cabinexchange.com

cabin exchange

Cabin Exchange is an annual artist-initiated event where four 2.4 x 3 metre containers are placed in the streets of Glasgow and Edinburgh. For a week each year this space is taken over by local and international artists and transformed, i.e. each artist receives three slots in one of the containers for a maximum of 24 hours to exhibit his or her work, which is generated from this context. It is a matter of creating a connection between the works of art and the locations, the residents and the artists, art and broader general public. Six artists from Great Britain act as curators of the project and to date have selected from among 400 artists nearly 120 site-specific works which cover a broad spectrum of media and themes, ranging from performances to exhibitions to theatre and readings. The participation of local residents is intended to have an influence on the final form of the project. In November 2005 the fourth Cabin Exchange week began with a decision about three areas with concrete locations. The artists involved then undertook 're-search time', at the end of which they created their container with special consideration of the needs, prejudices and structures of the particular neighbourhood. The containers were exhibited for an entire week in April 2006. The project's website served on the one hand as a way of documenting all of the works of art up to that point and on the other hand as a tool for communication in the form of blogs for the artists involved during the 'research time'. Urban space is a context which is only determined to a minimal degree from individuals. On the other hand, the placing of metal cubes in the city is a huge intervention which can provoke opposition. The containers, however, did not appear to cause such reactions, probably because they were perceived as temporary.

Title phonotaktik.02: The Social Construction of Technology

Type electronic music festival

Type of use cultural

Location phonotaktik 2002 Vienna played at the following locations:
Café Alt-Wien, Haus der Begegnung Mariahilf, Sportclub-
Platz (cemetery stage), Ares-Tower (19th to 21st storey),
ιters, Tenne,

May/June 2002

In
: Information

Temporary
Role

the scope of a
e realisation that
use for these
ally between elec-
tronic music and spatial metaphors and questions of space. These
relationships were to be picked up on as a central theme and
therefore unusual locations were chosen, each of which was only
used once or several times at most.

www.mond.at/phono; www.piknik.at

phonotaktik

Phonotaktik is a festival of electronic music in Vienna. From the beginning phonotaktik was an investigation of space within the city and went to locations not ordinarily intended for cultural events. The first festival, which occurred as part of the *80 Days of Vienna* architecture series in 1995, had no financial problems. Because phonotaktik could no longer be funded in 1997, however, it was converted at short notice into the *Picnic with Hermann* in the Hermannpark at the Vienna Danube Canal. In 1999 and 2002 the festivals went off normally, but in 2005 a reduced version was organised in a building pit in the new Donau-City neighbourhood and called *Picnic at the Wayside*. Although the official Vienna dresses itself up with the local electro-scene and the phonotaktik is famous in an international context, the event repeatedly fails due to budgetary problems. This might be due to the complex programme, but it is also because of the concept of the 'unknown location' as a site for the event and the unwieldy method of advanced ticket sales. In 1999 the organisers gained inspiration from Georg Franck's book *Die Ökonomie der Aufmerksamkeit* (The Economy of Attention) and distributed vouchers through a variety of channels with which it was possible to add one's name to the guest list on a website. Tickets were not sold in the conventional way. A similar method was used once again in 2002 and in addition the curators attempted to award the 50 festival invitations for musicians through the use of a participatory internet scheme. One could interpret phonotaktik as a tool for the formation of networks and for the varied use of sites. It calls on the city in a way that tells stories about this city unlike the usual ones. The festival allows for access to locations which would otherwise remain unknown and above all for uses which have nothing to do with the site's original purpose. Years after the first phonotaktik many visitors were able to remember the location of the event, but only a few could remember what music was played.

Title	Volxtheaterkarawane
Type	political street theatre
Type of use	social, cultural
Location	many European cities
Time	Volxtheater since 1994, Karawane since 2000
	in each case several hours to weeks
Initiator	Kollektiv Volxtheater
Temporary users	members of the Karawane, demonstration participants,
	passers-by
Role of city	none
Status	legal, the legality has been questioned by some
Goals	Central themes are examinations of racism, sexism,
	borders/limits, the control of migration and governmental
	surveillance.

no-racism.net/nobordertour
no-racism.net/noborderlab
no-racism.net
noborder.org

volxtheaterkarawane

The Volxtheater (People's Theatre) has been in existence since 1994, since a performance of *The Threepenny Opera* in the squatted Ernst-Kirchweger-Haus in Vienna. Its principles at that time were: no directors, no pay, the maximum possible collective decision-making and an open group-structure. From the very beginning activities in the theatre were linked to activities on the street, for instance actions against military parades and campaigns concerning refugee policies. When the conservative right-wing government took power in Austria at the beginning of 2000 the Volxtheater moved completely to the streets and took part in the various street protests occurring at the time. Central elements were the Volxküche (People's Kitchen), Propagandaradio, street duets, clowning, juggling and pie-throwing contests. Finally, in 2001, the Volxtheaterkarawane was started using the slogan 'no border – no nation.' The Karawane's (Caravan) goal was to make migration policy a major theme. Equipment and costumes consisted mostly of overalls, helmets, airbrushes and UN-soldiers' kit. These activities reached a peak with the group's participation in the demonstration for migrants' rights at the G8 Summit in Genoa in July 2001, where the Karawane was arrested. The Austrian Interior Ministry then made files of the group's members available to the Italian police in order to help incriminate the Karawane. They were charged with looting, vandalism, endangering public security and with forming a criminal organisation. The group's members were held in prison for three weeks but afterwards no charges were brought against them. In the following years a series of mobile projects about refugee policies was organised, for which a greater integration of audio-visual media at the events was striven for. An old English double-decker bus was made into a mobile media centre in 2002. Using it, the Volxtheaterkarawane went to the international noborder Camp in Strasbourg and to documenta11 in Kassel.

Title SOHO in Ottakring
Type art festival in a so-called 'urban problem area'
Type of use cultural

Location Ottakring, Gürtelnähe (Brunnenviertel), Vienna
Time annually since 1999, at the end of May/beginning of June
two weeks

Initiator Ula Schneider, artist
Temporary users in each case approximately 200 artists
Role of city sponsor
Status legal

Goals To create an alternative to the established art scene in the Brunnenviertal and improve communication in the neighbourhood, especially among resident artists and between them and other residents.

www.sohoinottakring.at

soho in ottakring

The Brunnenviertel, which is usually confronted with such problem-atical labels as commercial death, migrant's quarter and red light district, is an EU regional support area. SOHO in Ottakring is an urban neighbourhood project resulting from an artist's initiative and takes place in the Ottakring quarter, Vienna's sixteenth dis-trict. The centre of the district is the Brunnenmarkt, the longest street market in Europe. In continuous work, SOHO focuses on aspects of neighbourhood development, artistic intervention and possibilities of local participation. Its essential characteristics are cooperation with various local groups and with artists as well as the use of public space. The original interests were the opening up of resident artists' studios as well as the possibility of using empty bars for temporary exhibitions. Access orientated toward a broad spectrum of visitors soon aroused great interest. Because of the large number of empty business premises, the Economic Chamber viewed this project as an opportunity for 'revaluation' and became involved. In the meantime many shops had been rented once again and there was a 'top-down' interest in the continuation of the festival. The quarter was now in the middle of a process of gentrification and public interest in the area had grown. At this point new paths were being explored. If SOHO was to continue to exist it was necessary to change the content, structure and organi-sation, to intensify neighbourhood-related work and to reflect on the organisation's role within the area to a greater degree. Together with the artist Beatrix Zobl there was a relaunch in 2003, to better implement the concerns of the art project embedded in this neigh-bourhood. From a project purely concerned with exhibitions, a project which supported participatory artistic concepts developed to an increasing degree.

Title	Hotel Neustadt
Type	theatre festival in a prefabricated concrete housing estate
Type of use	cultural

Location	Halle-Neustadt, Germany
Time	March until October 2003, festival: 19 September to 2 October two weeks

Initiator	Thalia Theater Halle, Raumlabor Berlin
Temporary users	more than 100 youths for the hotel construction and operation, over 60 artists, festival visitors
Role of city	sponsor
Status	legal

Goals The goal was to win artists over who would work on artistic approaches to dealing with the restructuring of large but shrinking housing estates and the interests and wishes of the residents. Themes of the festival were living and life in general (especially in pre-fab estates), the hotel and urban planning processes and visions.

www.hotel-neustadt.de

hotel neustadt

Halle-Neustadt was the second biggest prefabricated concrete housing estate in the GDR. Based on a vision of a bright and shining city, Halle-Neustadt came into being after a period of construction that lasted 25 years. Beginning in 1963 and with the participation of international architects, a city for 100,000 inhabitants was created and richly endowed with social and urban infrastructure: department stores, schools, kindergartens, playgrounds, restaurants and a cinema. Halle-Neustadt in the autumn of 2003: 30% of flats vacant, 50% of residential buildings renovated, 25% unemployment, new facilities for the elderly and handicapped, vacant schools, hostels and shops, new automobile salesrooms, a new shopping centre, overgrown grounds, the first flats are being torn down. Hotel Neustadt is a vision that originated in the summer of 2003. Consisting of a hotel in a vacant tower block, which was planned, built and run by youth from the city of Halle with help of the Raumlabor Berlin, and an international theatre festival on the theme of 'Life in Large Housing Estates', which occurred in this very hotel. Hotel Neustadt was a different kind of festival, not a classical theatre-guest performance festival to which completed productions were invited. The festival concept was expanded upon in various respects – with respect to the location, the space, the participating artists, the visitors and the interaction. The hotel was the festival. Everything that occurred during the festival and everyone who was active belonged to the hotel: young people, artists who had been invited, the theatre and visitors. Balance sheets indicate that on average the hotel was booked-up 80% of the time with guests from around the world as well as from Halle. More than 100 youths were involved with the planning, the renovation of the rooms and the running of the hotel and club. There were over 60 happy artists who participated. It was a festival with many visitors, which is without equal, and not only in Halle. And, not to be forgotten, it revealed a great deal of development potential for Halle-Neustadt.

Balkontuning
Project by Peanutz Architekten

Title	ErsatzStadt
Type	making questions of urban public space a topic of discussion
Type of use	cultural
Location	Rosa-Luxemburg-Platz, in front of the Volksbühne theatre, Berlin, Germany
Time	end of June until middle of July 2003 16 days
Initiator	German Federal Cultural Foundation, Volksbühne
Temporary users	guests, participants
Role of city	none
Status	legal
Goals	With this project a virtual counterpart of an actual existing city was created, in which the subject of public and private space, the illegal occupation of land, gated communities and street vendors and shopping malls was discussed.

www.etuipop.de/ersatzstadt

ersatzstadt

ErsatzStadt began in 2002 as a project initiated by the German Federal Cultural Foundation in cooperation with the Volksbühne am Rosa-Luxemburg-Platz, and ended in the winter of 2005. The use of space, as it exists in every modern city, functioning mostly as niches for informal, perhaps even occasional illegal use, was illustrated. The project developed new pictures of the city and made suggestions for concrete, as well as utopian, improvements to urban life. ErsatzStadt produced various case studies (Lagos, Bombay, Istanbul, Rio de Janeiro, Buenos Aires, Kabul and Teheran), a temporary radio station, a mobile film-dialogue archive, theme weekends and workshops, a film documentation and a series of books. Part of the project was an exhibition in the summer of 2003 in connection with a public space for spontaneous settlement and unplanned activities on the occasion of the publication of the book *Hier entsteht: Strategien partizipativer Architektur und räumlicher Aneignung* (Under Construction: Strategies of Participatory Architecture and Spatial Appropriation) by Jesko Fezer and Mathias Heyden. A work-in-progress structure, which everyone could help build, was constructed on a property directly in front of the Volksbühne in Berlin. The name of this project was identical to the *Hier entsteht* publication. The dimensions, a floorspace of 200 m^2 and a height of 4.5 metres, were the only things pre-determined; all other planning decisions were delegated to those actively participating and were decided upon during construction. As a result of the temporary construction, the Volksbühne pavilion developed into a two-storey open platform which had a variety of uses. This building experiment offered space for exhibits, a reading room, a video cinema, a community information centre, lectures and discussions and also for unplanned and spontaneous activities. A lecture series with protagonists of participatory construction ran parallel to the exhibition.

Title Wochenklausur
Type socio-political, result-orientated interventions
Type of use socio-cultural

Location this example: Smart Museum, Chicago, USA, University of
Chicago; locations in Europe, USA and Japan
Time first from June to August 1993, 20 interventions since then
three to twelve weeks

Initiator Wolfgang Zinggl, artist, art theoretician
Temporary users Wochenklausur art group, social institutions
Role of city this example: none; with other projects: sponsor
Status legal

Goals The concept of intervention in the art world of today is, in a
somewhat inflationary way, applied to every kind of change.
Following the artists of the twentieth century, who understood
that they were to play a role in actively shaping society, the
Wochenklausur (Weeks in Conclave), in contrast, sees art as an
opportunity to bring about improvements in living together.
Design and creativity in traditional art applied mostly to formal
interests, but can also be employed to current problems in
education, ecology, the economy, urban planning and to social
tasks.

www.wochenklausur.at

wochenklausur

For short periods of time Wochenklausur uses the infrastructure and financial means of art institutions in order to initiate political and administrative problem-solving processes. Work is done on site for several weeks in order to solve a concrete problem. The first intervention in 1993 was the organisation of medical care for the homeless (instead of an exhibit in the Wiener Secession), using a bus which was converted into an ambulance. In 2005 the Smart Museum invited the Wochenklausur to use a project office at the University of Chicago for three weeks. The group dedicated itself during this time to the utilisation of material which accumulates at museums and theatres (glass cabinets, podiums, cloth and walls). Many of these materials are immediately thrown out at the end of an event. What one person considers rubbish is useful to someone else as material for everyday use. The group therefore built up a network: cultural institutions make their superfluous items available to social institutions which are lacking just such materials. In the socially underprivileged neighbourhood of Woodlawn, next to the campus, there were many institutions such as shelters for the homeless, soup kitchens and second-hand clothing shops which announced their need for furniture and practical items. At the same time theatres and museums were asked to make their unnecessary materials available and to join the network. The third group involved in this circulation system is comprised of design students. University design departments were brought on board in order to design and produce those items demanded in the future. During semester projects, students now build what the various institutions require. Their advantage is that they are able to carry out projects with no material costs. The project's actual goal was the establishment of an organisation called Material Exchange, which would take over the maintenance of the network on a long-term basis.

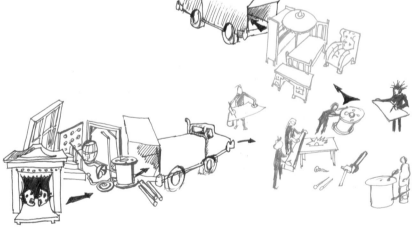

Title	Paris Plage
Type	city event
Type of use	entertainment

Location	the centre of Paris
Time	every summer since 2002
	four to five weeks each time, mid-July to mid-August

Initiator	Bertrand Delanoë, Mayor of Paris
Temporary users	four million visitors annually
Role of city	organiser
Status	legal

Goals	making city hall traffic policies a theme, summer entertainment

paris plage

At the initiative of Paris Mayor Bertrand Delanoë, the Georges Pompidou motorway in the city's centre has been replaced by a beach for four weeks every year since 2001. The beach lies on the right bank of the Seine between Pont Neuf and Pont de Sully. Because the river is not clean enough to swim in, a large temporary swimming pool is offered to visitors instead. Over a distance of 3.5 kilometres it is possible to lie in deck chairs and hammocks, go for a walk, play beach volleyball and visit cafés and concerts, as well as be cooled off by a fine mist from one of the popular *brumisateurs*. Approximately four million visitors come every year. For this purpose 3,000 tons of sand are poured onto the road, which is closed for the event. The project has an annual cost of two million euros, two-thirds of which are provided through sponsoring, and the occasion is a PR-event for the city hall's traffic policies, which envisage a future closing of the street. The idea has since been copied, without the political aspects, in a series of other European cities including Rome, Amsterdam, Berlin, Budapest, Prague and Vienna. In all of these cities the pure event therefore remains, which is certainly an essential sign of current urban policy in Europe and serves conversely, in the form of future event-like uses, exactly as a reason for urban planning decisions, instead of serving as a medium for urban planning suggestions which contain a social, cultural and, in any case, political background. The concept, incidentally, did not originate in Paris but in the small French city of St. Quentin, which has built a beach and swimming pool at the city hall plaza every summer since 1996.

Title	Nevidljivi Zagreb
Type	temporary cultural uses to support urban development
Type of use	cultural, planning
Location	Zagreb, Croatia
Time	since 2003
	from a number of hours to several months each time
Initiator	Platforma 9,81 – Udruga za arhitekturu i medije, NGO for architecture and media
Temporary users	event participants
Role of city	cooperation partner
Status	legal
Goals	The project concerns demanding citizen's rights of use as a prerequisite for all urban development. Non-institutional actors and the public administration are essential participants in this process.

www.platforma981.hr

nevidljivi zagreb

Deregulation and the decline of institutional power result in a social landscape of uncertainty. Although the spatial signs of the transition are visible on all levels, public planning departments are not able to follow the dynamics of these urban changes. A centralised planning model therefore represents a problem for urban development. Nevidljivi Zagreb (Invisible Zagreb) documents empty spaces in the city's transition and uses them for short-term cultural activities within the non-institutional scene. Many abandoned areas have been created as a result of empty factories and military bases as well as the end of public housing construction. The project investigates possibilities of informal urban policies, which will fill these spaces with temporary activities and denote a strategic delay, before the final change occurs. The goal is to investigate the city on an extensive scale, to categorise the spaces and, at the end of the project, make them usable for future architectural projects. The short-term activities are the beginning; the results of the workshops will be summarised and made available to those responsible in the city. The consequence of this could be to hold open competitions. Because of events held in an old listed slaughterhouse on Heinzelova Street this once again became part of a mental map of the city and is thus an example of how experience gained can be included in the city's planning culture. Bottom-up planning is a tool here and also the result of cooperation between the city administration and non-institutional initiatives. Croatia is the right country for this type of initiative because the scene there is very well organised and educated. The idea of achieving urban development through programmatic change is tied to the concept of mixed-use and informal micro-economies, which arise from such organisational principles.

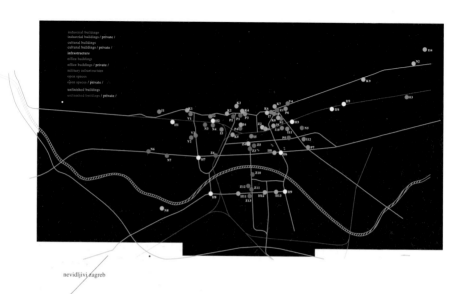

industrial buildings
industrial buildings / **private** /
cultural buildings
cultural buildings / **private** /
infrastructure
office buildings
office buildings / **private** /
military infrastructure
open spaces
open spaces / **private** /

unfinished buildings
unfinished buildings / **private** /

nevidljivi zagreb

PLATFORMA 9.81

left

Performance by BADCO. at Eurokaz festival, Nada Dimić factory

Tourist guide for squatters, Zagreb

right

Electronic music concert under Mladost bridge

Light installation "Red Empty" by Swedish artist Carl Michael von Hausswolff at Badel factory

Horvaćanska junction, presentation of the Croatian edition of "Empire" by Hardt/Negri

Title add on
Type art in public places
Type of use cultural

Location Wallensteinplatz, Vienna-Brigittenau
Time 18 June to 31 July 2005
six weeks

Initiator Peter Fattinger, Veronika Orso, Michael Rieper, architects
Temporary users all passers-by
Role of city sponsor (for the project submitted to the urban advisory board)
Status legal

Goals In various scenarios add on looks at basic human needs, such as living, sleeping and working in the interface between public and private spheres. As a reference to normal forms of living, these present their corresponding visual symbols externally. The interpreted exposure of functional units allows well-known processes to appear in a new context. Contradictory uses are a reaction to stereotypes of functionality and the social aspects linked with them are publicly negotiated.

www.add-on.at

add on

The accessible sculpture add on is one of the largest projects the Fonds zur Förderung von Kunst im öffentlichen Raum Wien (Funds for the Promotion of Art in Public Places in Vienna, founded in 2004) has ever supported. add on transformed Wallenstein-platz, with its *Gründerzeit* context, into a centre of artistic presentation for an entire summer. The basic structure of add on consists of a 20-metre high platform, into which space modules and inappropriately used prefabricated elements were interlocked. The environment thus created was generally accessible and invited people to 'explore urban life', allowing for a variety of internal and external views and vistas from its various levels. In a daily programme more than 20 artists demonstrated their respective positions within the interdisciplinary production of art and culture. The project's aesthetics cited architectural and sculptural works from the 1960s, ranging from urban utopias to alternative culture. Within this context, however, one has to question the context of its creation: It is not just an example of those non-elitist open art productions that go into people's neighbourhoods and serve as a counterweight to 'opera house culture'. It represents just as much an example of the event-orientated cultural policies of European cities, which emphatically seek out a more affluent class of cultural consumers without reverting to the conservative characteristics of the preceding generation – the much-quoted Bobos. Many contemporary art and architectural projects, however, have to live with this span of references, which refer to social aspects while employing them more as ornaments.

Title Creative Space Agency
Type agency for the procurement of temporarily available space for cultural industries
Type of use commercial

Location London
Time since April 2004
several weeks to more than a year each time

Initiators London Development Agency, Arts Council England
Temporary users creative industries
Role of city organisation of project
Status legal

Goals provision of cost-effective space for the creative industries

www.creativespaceagency.org.uk

creative space agency

The Creative Space Agency (CSA) is a new organisation which supports the creative industries, whose small-scale structure usually makes large expenditures for space impossible (but who nonetheless play an important economic role for cities), in their need for temporary spaces and buildings, no matter whether these are publicly or privately owned. Operations are presently being handled by Southwood Consultants in order to test their effectiveness and then to invite tenders for the full operation. Unused space will serve as a means of producing more events, exhibitions, performances and other creative activities, in order to help the Creative London Initiative make a contribution, so that London will remain the culturally interesting and creative city that it now is. The CSA is part of the Creative London Initiative. This type of organisation is especially important because, although London has an extremely active creative scene which employs more than 500,000 people (about 13% of all employees), the city also has extremely high rent costs which are a huge restriction for this branch. London's creative industries make more than 20 billion euros annually, more than any other industry, making this sector second only to business-related services. And they are just as dependent on central locations as the service industry. The CSA is active as a broker between owners and potential users from the creative industries. It runs a database of venues which is available online, has published a handbook concerning legal and practical conditions and offers sample contracts. For owners there is also a project database of those searching for space.

You can either search
by the following criteria

Name of borough
…

Size of space
…

Or

Press go to see
a complete list
of spaces

go

Barnet

Harrow

Brent

Hillingdon

Ealing

H + F

Hounslow

Wandsw

Richmond

Me

Kingston

Title Zwischenpalastnutzung
Type cultural use of a vacant building
Type of use cultural

Location Palast der Republik, Schlossplatz, Berlin, Germany
Time July 2003 until December 2005
a few hours to several months each time

Initiator Zwischen Palast Nutzung e.v. (Amelie Deuflhard, Joseph Hoppe, Philipp Oswalt, Philipp Misselwitz, Stefan Rethfeld, Eberhard Rhein, Gerriet Schultz, Jörn Weisbrodt)
Temporary users Volkspalast, Sophiensaele, HAU, Shrinking Cities, Urban Catalyst, Staatsoper Unter den Linden, WMF-Club, Partner für Berlin, Volksbühne, Fraktale, White Cube Berlin, etc.
Role of city none
Status legal

Goals Rediscovery and transformation of a formerly representative East German building located at the centre of the capital city. Updating a concept for use as a Volkspalast (people's palace) with a contemporary cultural programme. Moderation of a public debate to develop the site in a multi-facetted and forward-looking way.

www.urbancatalyst.de
www.zwischenpalastnutzung.de
www.palastbuendnis.de

zwischenpalastnutzung

In 2002 an international commission debated the future development of the Palace of the Republic site and reached the conclusion that the historic façade of the former palace should be reconstructed, behind which a new building containing the so-called Humboldt Forum would be built. This recommendation was supported by the German Bundestag. It is certain that construction of a new building will not begin before 2012. All asbestos was removed from the palace, which was not used after 1990, and simple safety measures were undertaken, so that the building stood as an empty shell in the centre of the city. This is why the idea of provisional use arose, accompanied by the fear that this would lead to a questioning of the building's demolition. In 2002 Urban Catalyst was commissioned to do a feasibility study on the building's provisional use. Although the results of this study were positive and broadly acknowledged, provisional use remained a controversial issue for some time. In 2003 a few guided tours, concerts, theatre productions and an exhibition were organised. Beginning in the summer of 2004 the Palace was made available for re-use as a people's palace. Among other projects the palace was flooded and a labyrinthine city consisting only of façades constructed. Guests could help shape the processes and appearance of the 'façade-republic'. At the 'Fun Palace Berlin 200X' convention, the venue's future was discussed with international architects. The accessible performance installation *People's Palace – the Mountain 2005* was a gigantic spatial installation, made possible by the involvement of over 100 artists. The centrepiece was a visitor-accessible mountain built inside the palace, which illustrated the discussion about how the building was being dealt with. By the end of 2005, 916 events had taken place within the framework of Zwischenpalastnutzung, with a total of 565,000 participants. The Palace of the Republic has since become a different building. Originally built as a form of legitimisation for a dictatorship, it stood for a longer period of time after the wall's removal than before. Demolition began in early 2006.

Fassadenrepublik
Project by Peanutz Architekten and
Raumlabor Berlin

Gasthof Bergkristall – Bergcamp
Project by Markus Bader and
Jan Liesegang, Raumlabor Berlin with
Alexander Römer

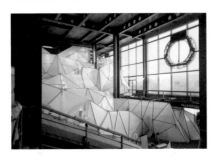

Title	einfach-mehrfach
Type	project coordination for multiple use
Type of use	cultural, sporting, social, entertainment

Location	spread throughout Vienna
Time	since April 1998
	partially long-term, partially provisional use for several months

Initiator	Jutta Kleedorfer, Urban Planning Department, Vienna
Temporary users	varied, mainly children and young people
Role of city	organisation of project
Status	legal

Goals The creation of open space, especially for children and young people, through the provisional and multiple employment of little-used areas.

www.wien.at/stadtentwicklung/06/22/01.htm

einfach-mehrfach

In the historic city and on the outskirts, open space, above all for children and young people, is becoming more and more scarce. For this reason the city of Vienna began the strategic project ein-fach-mehrfach (single-multiple), which is being managed by a coordinator without her own budget, who, by negotiating with public and private actors, tries to create open space by way of pro-visional and multiple-use strategies. On the one hand this concerns infrastructure like playgrounds and athletic facilities at public schools, which usually go unused evenings, weekends and holi-days, and which can be made available to the public at large. The project is also concerned with the interim use of vacant lots and unused areas, whereby owners' fears about liability problems are addressed because the city accepts responsibility for liability. The project is not only (but also) a form of social urban repair, but is also concerned with questions of democratic policy and with test-ing political participation at the local level. The project, with its specific basic conditions, is therefore situated between strategy and tactics, between improvisation and planning. An example of the project being put into action is the Mädchengarten (girls' gar-den) at an alternative music club's unused garden in Simmering, where girls are able to have their own place without having to defend it from attack. The garden also led to the girls once again going to public parks more often. The construction site play-ground in Leberberg, in a large urban development within the city, is an example of other directions the project goes in. After resi-dents moved into the area in the late 1990s hardly any open space remained and young people were forced to play in an under-ground car park. The city then took over the liability for a property reserved for a new shopping centre, and for an entire summer a 'construction site playground' was run as a better alternative to the car park.

Title	Kioskisierung
Type	temporary use of open space with kiosks in large housing estates
Type of use	architectural – urban planning
Location	Halle-Neustadt, Lódź-Retkinia, Bratislava-Petržalka, Moscow-Chertanovo
Time	June 2004 to September 2005 several years
Initiators	Benjamin Foerster-Baldenius, Jens Fischer, Peter Arlt, architects, sociologists
Temporary users	kiosk tour visitors and customers
Role of city	varied
Status	legal
Goals	The fundamental question was to what extent street vendors have taken hold and changed large housing estates and have therefore possibly had a stronger influence than urban planning and architectural interventions.

www.raumlabor.de
www.peterarlt.at

kioskisierung

In 2004 the Kioskisierung (kioskising) project investigated street vendors, using the example of kiosks in large housing estates in Halle-Neustadt, Lódź-Retkinia, Bratislava-Petržalka and Moscow-Chertanovo and went on tour through eastern Europe in September 2005 with the Kioskop, a small mobile kiosk-cinema. The project, sponsored by the German Federal Cultural Foundation, attempted to understand the current situation and development of street trading since the fall of communism, using the example of kiosks. In doing so those involved concentrated on large prefabricated concrete housing estates, which represent a special challenge for urban planners due to their monotony and mono-functionality. The connections between the existing built structure and these more or less improvised micro-economies were investigated: how they overlap, which ones disappear again and which new urban planning typologies originate from them. In Moscow's generously planned residential areas, for instance, there is enough open space available for the kiosks to grow into kiosk-conurbations and markets. The pinnacle of street vending was reached there in the mid-1990s. During the run-up to Moscow's 850-year anniversary in 1997 many kiosks were removed from the city's centre for the first time. At that time the city's politicians declared war against kiosks and markets. In Petržalka, Slovakia, there was a preference beginning in the mid-1990s for western banks, supermarkets and shopping malls. Large areas of development close to the centre of the city meant that a shopping mall zone could be created along the Einsteinnova bypass. In the Retkinia district of Lódź there have been as yet only a few scattered western supermarkets, which have allowed the structure that has arisen from the street to have a chance to develop the professionalism it needs in order to remain competitive with large chain stores.

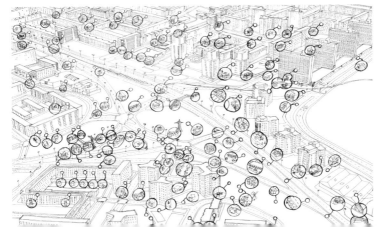

Title	OpTrek
Type	mobile project office
Type of use	cultural

Location	Transvaal district, The Hague, Holland
Time	August 2002 until autumn 2006
	four years

Initiator	Sabrina Lindemann, artist
Temporary users	very diverse, for the most part residents, and otherwise all interested parties
Role of city	sponsor
Status	legal

Goals	reflecting on urban renewal processes and making them more visible

www.optrektransvaal.nl

optrek

In the summer of 2002 a group of artists known as OpTrek moved into the multicultural district of Transvaal near the centre of The Hague. This part of the city will undergo extensive clearing and re-building over the next few years. OpTrek is concerned about the social and spatial changes caused by this plan and the consequences for residents. For four years OpTrek aimed at visualising the social and urban transformations in Transvaal for the general public by means of art. For this purpose artists and architects have been in-vited to create projects in public places. The restructuring of Trans-vaal is part of a global process in which cities compete with one another to present an attractive image. Centrally located areas built on expensive property, which are home to residents with low incomes, stand in the way of this. The mobile OpTrek project office takes on the role of a witness who reflects the complex local situa-tion and places it in a broader context of urban development pro-jects. In doing so the history of the district is recorded as well as the history of its residents. The office wanders from one empty building to the next, thereby serving as a base camp and meeting place. On average each stay at a new location lasts six months, at which time demolition makes relocation necessary. The façade of each office location is changed in order to make the presence of OpTrek obvious. In addition, each year six large projects are cre-ated in public places. These are supplemented by a series of smaller, spontaneous activities such as lectures and films. There are pro-jects at the district level aimed at the participation of residents as well as projects at the city level, which take place outside the district and throw light on the politics behind this urban restructur-ing. Reflecting on the position of the artists in the urban renewal process is an essential part of the entire project.

Title	Houthavens
Type	public art
Type of use	cultural

Location	former lumber harbour, Westerpark district, Amsterdam, Holland
Time	beginning in summer 2005
	approximately five years

Initiators	EN architecten, Stichting Werkspoor
Temporary users	users of the area
Role of city	none as of yet
Status	legal

Goals These interventions are intended as a way to analyse and observe the urban dynamism of this area, which currently finds itself between two planning identities. Inspiration for the future should thus be created during the ongoing planning interlude.

www.deverovering.com

houthavens

The area of the former Houthavens (lumber harbour), where until five years ago warehouses and DIY centres were located, is near the centre of Amsterdam, on the banks of the Ij River. Planning for new housing and small businesses was undertaken for the area and development began. Several years into this planning process one of the resident factories went to court to fight against the project and won, making a rethinking of the project necessary. The result is a pause of at least five years, within which the area, which has a rich historic identity, will have to wait for its future. People reacted spontaneously to this decision and began finding out about the character of the place. They colonised the land with planned and unplanned activities; they found opportunities for free parking and stealing cars or going for walks with the dog. Prostitutes offered their services and musicians practiced on their drums without disturbing the neighbours. Within a very short time the city's authorities began to put up fences and take control of the area. New uses such as an urban beach, temporary student housing in containers and a tour boat came into being in order to preserve the area's dynamism and give it a feeling of security. The project group was fascinated by the typical Dutch approach to planning, developing land, taking control and conquering and for this reason they named the planned project de *Verovering* (the conquest). At the beginning there was a series of small interventions: people were asked to sow poppy seeds in order to give the area more colour, to celebrate it and to reduce visibility of the fences. Two observatories were built to allow for another perspective of the area. At present the group is trying to find financial support in order to fund future interventions such as a large observation tower, for example.

de verovering

berat klaprozenmad

kijk
luister
ruik
verken
verover
de houthavens

kom zaaien
kleur
de houthavens
20 mei . 17 uur

www. de verovering .com

Title bed by night
Type accommodation for homeless youths
Type of use social

Location system of 14 Containers, Hanover, Germany
Time since August 2002
planned to last five to ten years

Initiator City of Hanover
Temporary users approximately 150 homeless youths
Role of city support and organisation of project
Status legal

Goals offering homeless youths places to sleep and eat and
looking after them

www.bed-by-night.de

bed by night

Experts estimate that there are between 2,000 and 50,000 children and young people between the ages of eight and eighteen living on the streets in Germany. They have lost contact with their families and live illegally. In Hanover there are approximately 150 children who have no contact with their parents and fend for themselves. In order to take care of them the project bed by night was started in the state capital Hanover. bed by night offers these children a place where they find rest and protection, where they will be taken seriously and accepted without any formalities. They can get a meal, wash their clothes and spend the night. The trained staff members are available at any time for discussions, advice and care. Since its opening in 1996 about 600 different children and youths have come to bed by night; more than two-thirds were able to leave life on the streets behind them. The containers, which were originally used for war refugees, were not in use anymore and architect Han Slawik, who had long worked with the construction of containers, was commissioned to create new facilities. Using two two-storey stacks of containers with a total of 21 elements, he designed a ground floor that contains offices and conference rooms, a lounge and cooking and eating areas, and an upper storey with sleeping areas and sanitary facilities, all covered with an exterior glass skin. Containers from the old facility were repaired and reused to build the new structure. The facility is open around the clock 365 days a year and the door is open until 11 pm for the children and youths who wish to sleep there. The building is located in a small park on Celler Straße and looks unconventional and striking thanks to its intensive colour scheme, which certainly suits its purpose. The question remains as to why the city administration only offers street children a series of containers instead of a permanent building. The main idea of the project is obviously to send a signal of temporariness.

Title	Squatting
Type	residing
Type of use	social, cultural

Location	many European cities, e.g. in Berlin, Hamburg and Amsterdam
Time	since the early 1970s
	from a few hours to many years

Initiators	flat-hunters
Temporary users	flat-hunters, guests at events
Role of city	varied
Status	illegal, later partially legal

Goals	Motives for squatting are above all the wish for a free place to live, the lack of a flat or even homelessness and protest against speculative vacancy and high rents.

squatting

The squatters' symbol, a circle with an N-shaped lightning bolt, originally came from the *Zinken* (thieves' sign language) for 'one can spend a night here'; the N stands for *neemt* (occupied). The symbol was first used in the Dutch squatters' scene during the 1970s, which was also known as *Kraaker*. Squatting began in West Germany in the late 1970s and early 1980s, especially in Berlin (at its peak there were more than 160 squatted houses there) and Hamburg, but also in many other cities. Squatting in Berlin-Kreuzberg, which was primarily connected with protest against large-scale urban redevelopment, manifested itself in so-called 'maintenance-squatting' and finally led to a social legitimisation of the principle of urban renewal. In fact, most of the Kreuzberg squats were ended by city authorities by 1981, after the scene became divided due to a few 'legalisations'. The manifestations and demonstrations linked to squatting greatly determined housing policies as well as housing practices in Germany. As with urban renewal, the concept of 'residential projects'(which were self-planned, organised and administered), which began during the 1980s, also stemmed from squatting. These projects involved privately and commonly initiated renovations or newly constructed buildings with the claim of being a community, which expressed itself in both spatial and social structures. Many such projects arose from specific user-groups which wanted to fashion their residential environments to the greatest possible extent, for example in the shape of women's residential projects. The centres of the squatting principle were above all the Netherlands, Germany and Switzerland, but there were, and still are, squatted buildings in many other European countries, which is not the case in the USA. Many of those buildings in Germany and the Netherlands which were originally squatted have since been legalised. There are, however, buildings which have not been formally legalised, but are merely unofficially tolerated.

Title	Giardino dell'Ararat, Campo Boario
Type	art and Kurdish cultural centre, accommodation for immigrants
Type of use	cultural, social
Location	former slaughterhouse (mattatoio), Rome, Italy
Time	Stalker started as a group of architecture students in the early 1990s, the use of Campo Boario started in 1999 it began seven years ago
Initiators	Stalker in cooperation with the Kurdish immigrant community, artists, architects and students
Temporary users	immigrants as residents, Stalker's office; the events are open to the public
Role of city	none
Status	illegal
Goals	Preservation of the unofficially used industrial area for flats and cultural facilities for and by immigrants, those here legally as well as illegally.

www.stalkerlab.it

242   **giardino dell'ararat**

Stalker is a collective consisting of architects, landscape planners, artists and others, named after the film by Tarkovsky and founded at the beginning of the 1990s, when radical Italian student movements were at their peak. The first Stalker project was a five day *dérive* through the Roman periphery. Its forerunners were groups like Archigram, Superstudio, Archizoom and Ufo during the 1960s and experimental architects like Cedric Price. Stalker also cites Situationism and its theories. The collective works with urban interim space, the migration of non-European cultures, urban social mobility and life-styles, area-specific interventions and new forms of media. In 1999, on the occasion of Venice's biennial for young European and Mediterranean artists, Stalker was commissioned with a workshop in Rome and as a part of this project transformed the Campo Boario, a former slaughterhouse in southern Rome directly on the Tiber's left bank and just inside the Aurelian city walls. The area had been taken over by immigrants since its closure 30 years before and during the workshop was turned into Ararat, a cultural centre for Kurdish immigrants. Workshop participants, among them architecture students and immigrants, began to alter the empty building for its use as Ararat and for residential use by the communities involved. With the help of an effectively publicised ideas competition with a prominent jury, attention was drawn to this project in 2000, thus preventing planned evictions. The area is still being used, has residents and is home to art and cultural events. Continuous renovation is carried out by the users and a Roma camp has also developed there. Work is ongoing to establish links between the communities living there as well as to create an opening to the city of Rome without commercialising the area.

Title	SchoolParasites
Type	temporary, cost-effective additions for schools built during the 1950s and 1960s
Type of use	social
Location	Hoogvliet, Rotterdam, Holland
Time	since May 2004
	several years
Initiator	WIMBY! International Building Exhibition Rotterdam
Temporary users	pupils and teachers
Role of city	financial support
Status	legal
Goals	cost-effective but architecturally high-quality spatial extensions for post-war schools

www.schoolparasites.nl

schoolparasites

The SchoolParasites are alternative emergency classrooms for schools in the Hoogvliet area built during the 1950s. Many such temporary school additions have been built in the Netherlands, but most of them are of inferior architectural quality. This is supposed to be different in Hoogvliet: the pavilions should be cost-effective but nonetheless offer spatial quality, thus improving the existing school. The new rooms can serve as classrooms but are mainly intended to be used for new activities, for instance the 'Beast' is used for making music and dancing, the 'Flower' offers space which can be divided into six small rooms for discussions and private lessons, and the 'Chinese Lantern' is used for cooking and eating. The Parasites have been developed for mass production and can therefore be ordered by and built at every Dutch school at any time. Three prototypes were introduced in May 2004: the 'Chinese Lantern', designed by industrial designer Christoph Seyferth and built at the Tuimelaar Elementary School, the 'Flower' by architect Barend Koolhaas, built at the De-Notenkraker School and the 'Beast' by the architecture office Onix, built at the Jacobus School. These anonymous post-war schools also have an identity and history, which reflects the architectural history as well as the social development of the suburb. The architects have made a virtue out of necessity, which in this case was a lack of money and space. Using minimal interventions they have proven the plausibility of an urban planning improvement strategy that does not react with radical large-scale measures, but reduces, if not removes, concrete deficits unpretentiously and at reasonable cost. The project is part of the WIMBY! (Welcome Into My Backyard!) International Building Exhibition Rotterdam-Hoogvliet, which was managed by Crimson Architectural Historians and received the Dutch Design Award in 2004.

248

Title	Community Gardens
Type	community gardens in New York
Type of use	social

Location	more than 800 gardens throughout New York City; at present approximately 750 still exist
Time	since 1973
	average useful life of a garden: nine years, some have lasted more than 30 years

Initiators	self-organised neighbourhood groups
Temporary users	local residents, open to the public at large; almost 20,000 garden members, approximately ten to twenty per garden; between ten and more than 1000 visitors per garden
Role of city	property owner: the Parks Department runs Operation Green Thumb, which leases land and supports gardeners
Status	legal, sometimes merely tolerated

Goals	the creation of areas for rest and relaxation in neglected urban neighbourhoods as well as the possibility of planting vegetables and fruit
	www.greenguerillas.org
	www.alliedproductions.org

community gardens

In New York working gardens already existed during the depression, as did victory gardens during the Second World War, but it was not until the 1970s that gardens were first organised by users themselves. At this time a tax crisis led to urban decline and it was feared that vacant properties belonging to the city would become centres of drugs, prostitution and crime – or, from the opposite perspective: the politics of 'spatial deconcentration' after the large race riots during the 1960s left empty police and fire stations, bank branch offices and, for the purpose of receiving insurance payments, burnt out buildings in their wake. In 1973 the Green Guerillas, a self-organised group of residents and artists, began cleaning up the first of many publicly owned properties on the Lower East Side of Manhattan and converting them into gardens. Many other activists followed this example, at first in the Lower East Side and ultimately in all of the city's five boroughs, so that in 1978 the city administration initiated Operation Green Thumb, which leases land to community gardeners using quickly terminable contracts costing one dollar per year, if those in charge of the gardens recognise that the property belongs to the city and not to them. In 1994 the new mayor, Rudy Giuliani, decided to auction off properties used as community gardens, although at the same time there would have been thousands of unused public properties. The Garden Preservation Coalition was founded in order to fight against this. In 2000 Guiliani said, 'If you live in an unrealistic world then you can say everything should be a community garden.' There are now about 750 community gardens in New York City, most of them leased with quickly terminable contracts, even though several of the gardens have been dedicated as permanent parks.

Title ABC No Rio

Type neighbourhood centre and gallery for alternative art, activism, concerts and performances

Type of use cultural, social

Location 156 Rivington Street, Lower East Side, New York City, USA

Time since 1980

26 years

Initiators artists in New York City from the Colab milieu, an artists' collective during the 1970s and 1980s

Temporary users local neighbourhood groups, youth fringe groups, artists, activists; approximately 100 volunteer helpers

Role of city the city owns the building and agreed to sell it to ABC No Rio in 1997 for one dollar, provided that fundraising for the building's restoration was started and that the building would remain dedicated to public use; exhibits are partially supported by the NY State Council on the Arts

Status illegal to semi-legal, with the prospect of becoming legal

Goals The creation of affordable space for cultural and social uses

www.abcnorio.org

ABC No Rio is an art centre in the Lower East Side located in a previously empty building belonging to the city. ABC No Rio was founded by artists who pursue political and social activism and is known as a place of oppositional culture and punk. On New Year's Eve in 1979 around 30 artists occupied an empty building with an exhibition entitled *The Real Estate Show,* in order to protest the city's housing and land use policies and to promote 'insurgent urban development'. After police broke up the exhibition on New Year's Day the city began to negotiate with the artists, which finally resulted in them giving up the building they had been using in exchange for another one. This building had already been squatted before the collective legally took over the ground floor and began paying a slight rent to the city. Since then No Rio has been the scene of exhibitions, performances, readings, films, punk shows, experimental music performances as well as courses in drawing, photography and film making for adolescents. There is a dark room, a printing studio, a computer centre and the Zine Library, one of the largest collections of underground publications. In 1994 the city planned to vacate the building and sell it to a non-profit developer who wanted to build low-income flats there. In 1997, after three years of negotiations, the NYC Department of Housing, Preservation and Development promised to sell the building to ABC No Rio provided that the squatted upper storeys were cleared out and the centre enlarged. Furthermore, 100,000 dollars were to be collected so that the building could be restored in accordance with building codes. A restoration in three phases eventually took place over the next few years, with a budget of over 350,000 dollars. The contract with the city was never concluded, however, and for that reason No Rio remains in a semi-legal state.

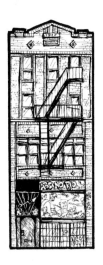

Title	Kulturzentrum Arena
Type	events-collective
Type of use	cultural

Location	former domestic market slaughterhouse in Vienna
Time	a movement since 1970, an association since 1974, slaughterhouse since 1976, legalisation in 1980
	30 years up to now

Initiator	autonomous cultural promoter
Temporary users	visitors at events
Role of city	property owner; has subsidised the operation since 1998, financial support for the current adaptations
Status	now legal (since 1977 verbal agreement)

Goals	the establishment of an autonomous cultural centre, especially for adolescents, in Vienna

www.arena.co.at

arena

During the legendary hot summer of 1976 the St. Marx export market slaughterhouse (which had an area of 70,000 m²) was to be used one last time for a series of non-mainstream events entitled *Arena* as part of the Vienna festival and then demolished (the name Arena referred to the arrangement of seating for the audience). The 'Arenauts', a group of cultural workers, intellectuals, social workers and students, but also numerous young workers, unemployed persons and drop-outs, tried to prevent this by occupying the area and forcing the establishment of a self-administered cultural centre. The squatters stood firm throughout the summer, but in the end were removed and the area torn down. The city of Vienna, however, offered them the neighbouring domestic market slaughterhouse as an alternative, which is only 7,600 m² in size. After an initial phase of rejecting the alternative proposal, a cultural establishment was begun in a more or less squatter-like manner in 1977, but was made legal in 1980 due to pressure from a 'new' youth movement. Today the Arena is an alternative centre for events which has several stages and pubs and an open-air cinema, and is subsidised by the city. Several of those who had lived in the original Arena continued their programme in squatted houses in Vienna (Gassergasse, Ägidigasse). Another subsequent project is Club Flex, which was first run in a pub in Meidling but had to move on after five years because of constant problems with residents there. Since 1994 Flex has been in a previously unused underground tunnel next to the banks of the Danube Canal and is thus located in the centre of Vienna. And finally, the Vienna newspaper *Falter* should be mentioned as another resultant project. The Arena's brick structure, built during the *Gründerzeit* (period of rapid expansion between 1850 and 1914) and partially listed, has been gradually restored over the past few years, in order to reduce noise pollution for neighbours and to improve the conditions for running concerts.

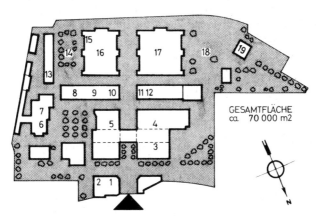

160

GESAMTFLÄCHE
ca 70 000 m2

N

1	SELBSTVERWALTUNGS-GEBÄUDE (REDAKTION, ARBEITSGRUPPEN)	6	HAUS SIMMERING	13	SOLDATENHAUS
2	SANITÄT	7	DISCOTHEK	14	LAGERWIESE
3	FILMPALAST	8	CAFÉ 'SCHWEINESTALL'	15	KÜCHE
4	THEATERHALLE	9	ROTE HALLE	16	GROSSE HALLE
5	VIDEO UND DIA	10	TEEHAUS	17	GALERIE
		11	LITERATENCAFÉ	18	SPIELWIESE
		12	FRAUENHAUS	19	KINDERHAUS

4/5

Peter Arlt
is a freelance sociologist focusing on the field of 'public space':
research, plans, actions, temporary buildings. Since 2004 he has been
guest professor at the Kunstuniversität Linz and a member of the board
of the Architekturforum Oberösterreich. Additional information at
www.peterarlt.at. Selected projects: Bad Ly: Public swimming pool in
portable building containers, Berlin, 1999; Kongress der Straßen-
expertinnen, Linz, 2001; Platz finden: neighbourhood competition with
public square reorganisation, in cooperation with public works and
G. Heidecker, Linz 2004–05; Kioskisierung: research project with
B. Foerster-Baldenius and J. Fischer, 2004–05.

Friedemann Derschmidt
freelance artist and filmmaker, who is currently working on a film
about the founders of the Web caster Gipsyradio, directs the Institut zur
Erforschung und Erschaffung von Ritualen und Zeremonien (institute
for rites and ceremonies). The creator of Permanent Breakfast: The Continuous Breakfast in Public Space, an art action in public space following
the principles of the social sculpture. Selected films: *Komm und sieh
Rudyn: Geschichten eines Tänzers aus Wien,* 1999, with Walter Pucher;
Spurensuche – Raumordnungen on the Austrian-Czech border, 2006,
with Sonja Ceijka, Karin Schneider and Abbe Libansky.

Florian Haydn
architect and urbanist; lives and works in Vienna; co-founder of the
POOR BOYS ENTERPRISE. Awarded the prize for experimental trends in
architecture (Preis für Experimentelle Tendenzen in der Architektur),
1996, participated in the exhibition *Archilab 2000,* Orléans; various
competition prizes (e.g., first prize "Stadt 2000, KDAG Wien"; first prize
"EUROPAN 8, Schwechat/Wien"); project partner in the EU-funded research project Urban Catalyst, on temporary strategies in urban planning;
publications on urbanistic themes (e.g., in the journals *dérive* and *hinter-
grund* and in the volume *Die Beute Stadt,* ed. the POOR BOYS ENTERPRISE,
Vienna, 1995). In 2005, he co-founded 000y0 with Georg Böhm and
Mirko Pogoreutz. www.000y0.at.

biographies

Ursula Hofbauer
scholar of landmarks, born 1964, studied architecture in Vienna.
Member of Alltag und Geschichte: Verein zur Erforschung populärer
Kultur und öffentlicher Räume (quotidian and history: association for
research on popular culture and public spaces), among others in the
1998 exhibition *strange views,* on the theme of ethnological shows in
Vienna's Prater park. Founding member of the Permanent Breakfast
association. Idea, organisation and implementation of the first Vienna
wine tasting for the homeless, under the Schwedenbrücke, as part
of Permanent Breakfast (2002). Until September 2004 she worked in
various architectural offices.

Barbara Holub
visiting professorship at the University of Illinois at Chicago, School of
Art and Design, 1997. Most recent publication: *Barbara Holubs Muster-
buch: Ideal Living* (Vienna, 2003); 2004 Schindler Scholarship, MAK
Center for Art and Architecture, Los Angeles; since 2004 on the Beirat
für Kunst im öffentlichen Raum Niederösterreich. In 1999 she founded
transparadiso with Paul Rajakovics. Selected projects: *Secession,* Vienna,
1999; *Gouvernementalität,* Alte Kestner-Gesellschaft, Hanover, 2000;
Common Ground, Shared Place, Galerija Marino Cettina, Umag, 2001;
In einer Wohnlandschaft herrscht kein Bilderverbot, Galerie Hohenlohe &
Kalb, Vienna, 2003. www.transparadiso.com

Christa Kamleithner
studied architecture at the University of Technology Vienna and philos-
ophy at the University of Vienna. Writer and editor for *dérive: Zeitschrift für Stadtforschung,* 2000–04; member of the board of the Österreichische Gesellschaft für Architektur (Austrian Architectural Society),
since 2001. Participant in the EU research project Urban Catalyst:
Strategies for Temporary Use, 2003. Project associate at the University of
Technology Graz, 2004–05; assistant professor at the Berlin University
of the Arts since 2006.

Rudolf Kohoutek
studied architecture at the University of Technology Vienna and
geography at the University of Vienna. Research, texts and lectures on
architecture, dwelling, urban development, culture and planning

methods since 1971. Co-founder of Urbane Initiativen. Participant in the EU research project Urban Catalyst: Strategies for Temporary Use in 2003. Works freelance in Vienna.

Elke Krasny
is a cultural theorist, author and exhibition curator who teaches cultural pedagogy at the Academy of Fine Arts Vienna and writes for *Architektur aktuell.* Selected exhibitions: *Von Haus zu Haus: Private Architektur im öffentlichen Raum* at the Architekturzentrum Wien, 1997; *Welt Ausstellen: Schauplatz Wien,* 1873 at the Museum of Technology Vienna, 2004; and *www.musieum.at: Displaying Gender.* Emphases: everyday spaces and fiction, representation and gender, museums and exhibitions as manifestations of designed cultural communication, urban space and participatory approaches.

Mirko Pogoreutz
born in Leipzig, in 1972, raised in Thuringia, professional wanderings, then between 1995 and 2000 studied architecture and urban development in Potsdam and Milan; participant in Urban Catalyst in Vienna, 2002–03; co-organiser of the symposium 'tempo..rar' in Vienna, 2003; participated in numerous competitions on urban planning themes in various ways; urban interventions such as Suhl: ? Stadt; co-founded 000y0 in 2005 with Georg Böhm and Florian Haydn.

Paul Rajakovics
transbanana architects, 1996–99; dissertation *Kontextuelles Handeln in Architektur und Städtebau* (Contextual Action in Architecture and Urban Development), 2001; member of the editorial board of *dérive: Zeitschrift für Stadtforschung* since 2001; works for Europan Österreich since 2004. Schindler Scholarship, MAK Center for Art and Architecture, Los Angeles, 2004. Founded transparadiso with Barbara Holub, 1999. Selected projects: deseo urbano, Valparaiso, Chile, 2000–01; from 2001–02, access.all.areas, lead project for Jugendkultur, Kulturhauptstadt Graz 2003; one in a million, Austrian Cultural Forum, New York, 2004; Indikatormobil, MAK Wien, 2005. www.transparadiso.com

Klaus Ronneberger
born 1950, studied social pedagogy, cultural studies and sociology. He worked for many years for the Institut für Sozialforschung (Institute for Social Research) in Frankfurt am Main and today works as a freelance journalist. He was a member of the urban research group SpaceLab and for Nitribitt: Frankfurter Ökonomien. Selected publications: *Die neue Dienstleistungsstadt: Berufsmilieus in Frankfurt am Main* with Peter Noller (1995), *Die Stadt als Beute* with Stephan Lanz and Walther Jahn (1999).

Andreas Spiegl
studied art history at the Universtiy of Vienna and since 1990 has taught in the department for theory, practice and mediation of contemporary art at the Academy of Fine Arts Vienna, serving as Vice Rector for Theory and Research since 2003. His research focuses on questions of the theory of space seen from various perspectives, such as media theory, architecture theory, feminism and psychoanalysis. In 1999 he co-founded the Büro für kognitiven Urbanismus with Christian Teckert.

Christian Teckert
born in Linz in 1967, studied architecture at the Academy of Fine Arts Vienna. Since 1992, projects and publications at the intersection of art, urbanism, space theory and architecture as well as interdisciplinary projects and articles such as video productions, theoretical works, publications, exhibitions, lectures and architecture. In 1999 he co-founded the Büro für kognitiven Urbanismus with Andreas Spiegl. In 2001 he co-founded AS-IF architekten with Stephanie Kaindl and Paul Grundei in Berlin and Vienna. Most recent project: exhibition building for the Galerie für Zeitgenössische Kunst in Leipzig.

Robert Temel
is architectural critic and theoretician in Vienna as well as Chair of the Österreichische Gesellschaft für Architektur (ÖGFA, Austrian Architectural Society). A central theme of his interest in the spatial environment is public space and its use – that was, among other things, the subject of the symposium 'tempo..rar: Temporäre Nutzungen im Stadtraum', which he organised in 2003 with Florian Haydn.

We owe thanks to many people for this volume.

First of all, to our co-organiser, Mirko Pogoreutz; the photographer Nina Dick and the participants in the conference 'tempo..rar: Temporäre Nutzungen im Stadtraum' in Vienna in May 2003: Peter Arlt, Sabine Breitfuss, Gerhard Buresch, Jens Dangschat, Friedemann Derschmidt, Ron Eizenstain, Andreas Feldkeller, Martin Fritz, Matthew Griffin, Hans Groiss, Ursula Hofbauer, Barbara Holub, Brigitte Jilka, Christa Kamleithner, Jutta Kleedorfer, Rudolf Kohoutek, Elke Krasny, Martin Kutschera, Michael Mellauner, Helmut Mondschein, Klaus Overmeyer, Erich Petuelli, Sabine Pollak, Paul Rajakovics, Christian Reder, Walter Rohn, Klaus Ronneberger, Florian Schmeiser, Andreas Schneider, Roland Schöny, Georg Schöllhammer, Dieter Schreiber, Susanne Schuda, Martin Schwanzer, Andreas Spiegl, Dietmar Steiner, Christian Teckert, Klaus Vatter, Rudolf Zabrana, Wolfgang Zinggl and Beatrix Zobl.

We are also grateful to those who gave money and supported the conference: Bundeskanzleramt.Kunst, MA 7 – Kulturamt der Stadt Wien and the Architekturzentrum Wien.

In addition, we would like to thank our predecessor project, Urban Catalyst, and its project directors, Klaus Overymeyer, Philipp Oswalt and Philipp Misselwitz and all the project partners in Berlin, Naples, Helsinki, Amsterdam and Vienna. We are also grateful to those who gave us an opportunity to present and discuss sketches and ideas in the run-up to this publication, especially the Architekturzentrum Wien; the journal *dérive: Zeitschrift für Stadtforschung* and its editor, Christoph Laimer; the architecture gallery Framework; the Aktionsradius Augarten and the Theatercombinat with Firma Raumforschung in Vienna.

We owe thanks to the authors of the present volume and to Alexandra Wachter, who supported us with project research, and then to all the informants for the project documentation: Peanutz Architekten, Georg Böhm, Michael Hueners (Radioballett), Annemarie Burckhardt, Martin Schmitz (Spaziergangswissenschaft), Space Hijackers, Ursula Hofbauer, Friedemann Derschmidt (Permanent Breakfast), Marion Hamm (Reclaim the Streets!), Glas (Urban Cabaret), Florian Schmeiser, Susanne Schuda

acknowledgements

(kein Geld, instant island), Christian Lagé (kraut), Jesko Fezer (Camp for Oppositional Architecture, ErsatzStadt), Florian Gass, Club Real (Traumkombinat), Will Foster (Cabin Exchange), Hans Groiß (phono-taktik), Gini Müller (Volxtheaterkarawane), Ula Schneider, Beatrix Zobl (SOHO in Ottakring), Raumlabor Berlin (Hotel Neustadt, Zwischen-palastnutzung), Wolfgang Zinggl (Wochenklausur), Sylvie Vermeulen (Paris Plage), Marko Sancanin (Nevidljivi Zagreb), Michael Rieper, Peter Fattinger (add on), Jules Nurrish (Creative Space Agency), Stefan Rethfeld (Zwischenpalastnutzung), Jutta Kleedorfer (einfach-mehrfach), Peter Arlt (Kioskisierung), Sabrina Lindemann (OpTrek), Hanneke van Wel (Houthavens), Han Slawik (bed by night), Philipp Haydn (Community Gardens, ABC No Rio), Dieter Schrage (Kultur-zentrum Arena). We are, of course, responsible for any errors or inaccuracies that remain.

Finally, we thank the Birkhäuser publishers, especially Karoline Mueller-Stahl and Robert Steiger, Richard Ferkl and Jo Schmeiser for layout and typesetting, and those who gave money for the publication: Bundeskanzleramt.Kunst, Bundesministerium für Bildung, Wissenschaft und Kultur, and MA 7 – Kulturamt der Stadt Wien, Abteilung Wissen-schaftsförderung.

Florian Haydn and Robert Temel

Texts

Spaces for Action and for
Laughing Too
Peter Fattinger, P 83
Hiroko Inoue, P 84
Richard V. Strauss, P 88

Vacancies and Urban Reserves
transparadiso, P 116-117

Projects

Radioballett, P 124-125
Eiko Grimberg

1	2
	3
	4

Spaziergangswissenschaft,
P 128-129
Fachbereich Stadtplanung /
Landschaftsplanung, GhKassel: 1
Klaus Hoppe: 2
Armin Okulla: 3, 4

Circle Line Party, P 132-133
Space Hijackers

1	5	8	11
2	6		12
3		9	13
4	7	10	14

Permanent Breakfast, P 136-137
Friedemann Derschmidt: 1, 6
Christian Smretschnig: 2
Abbe Libansky: 3, 10, 14
Andreas Gartner: 4
Folkard Fritz: 5
Carla Bobadilla: 7, 8
Leo Sauermann: 9
Laura Mello: 11
Heinrich Reinhart: 12
Philipp Mayrhofer: 13

Reclaim the Streets!, P 140-141
Johannes Grönvall

Urban Cabaret, P 144-145
Glas

1	2	3
		4

kein Geld, P 148-149
Susanne Schuda: 1
Florian Schmeiser: 2, 4
Christa Ziegler: 3

photo credits

<table>
<tr><td>1</td><td>5</td></tr>
<tr><td>2 3</td><td>4 6</td></tr>
</table>

instant island, P 152-153
Florian Schmeiser: 1-4
Christa Ziegler: 5 (from the
photoseries "Praterstern")
Marie Jecel: 6

kraut, P 156-157
anschlaege.de

Camp for Oppositional
Architecture, P 160-161
Daniel Wilkniß, Beate Fiegle,
An Architektur

<table>
<tr><td>1 3</td><td>4 5</td></tr>
<tr><td>2</td><td>6</td></tr>
</table>

Hirnsegel #7, P 164-165
Norbert Artner: 1, 2
Bruno Stubenrauch: 3, 5
Florian Haydn: 4, 6

<table>
<tr><td>1</td><td>2 6
3 7
4
5 8</td></tr>
</table>

Traumkombinat, P 168-169
Club Real: 1-3, 5, 6
Hannes Rascher: 4, 7
Hedi Lusser: 8

Cabin Exchange, P 172-173
Cabin Exchange

<table>
<tr><td>1</td><td></td><td>5</td></tr>
<tr><td>2</td><td>4</td><td>6</td></tr>
<tr><td>3</td><td></td><td>8</td></tr>
<tr><td></td><td></td><td>7</td></tr>
</table>

phonotaktik, P 176-177
phonotaktik: 1-6, 8
Marika Rakoczy: 7

<table>
<tr><td></td><td>2</td><td>4 8</td></tr>
<tr><td>1</td><td></td><td>5 9</td></tr>
<tr><td></td><td></td><td>6 10</td></tr>
<tr><td></td><td>3</td><td>7 11</td></tr>
</table>

Volxtheaterkarawane, P 180-181
Festival der Regionen /
noborderlab: 1-4, 8
noborderlab: 5-6, 9-11
noborderzone: 7

SOHO in Ottakring, P 184-185
Götz Bury

```
 1        4  7
 2   3    5  8
             9
          6
```

Hotel Neustadt, P 188-189
Gert Kiermeyer: 1, 7
Grotest Maru: 2
Annett Jummrich: 3
Matthias Rick: 4, 9
Benjamin Foerster-Baldenius: 5
Peanutz Architekten: 6
Annett Jummrich: 8

ErsatzStadt, P 192-193
Katja Eydel,
Mathias Heyden,
Jesko Fezer,
Tim Müller-Heidelberg

Wochenklausur, P 196-197
WochenKlausur

```
 1        | 5
 2        |
    3     |
    4     |
```

Paris Plage, P 200-201
Karl Petersen: 1
Marjorie Guilbaud / Mairie
de Paris: 2
Sophie Robichon / Mairie
de Paris: 3
Selina Ebert /
www.blog-art.com: 4
Antoine Magne: 5

```
 1        4  6
          5  7
             8
 2   3       9
```

Nevidljivi Zagreb, P 204-205
Platforma 9.81: 1-3, 6, 8, 9
Sandro Lendler: 4, 5, 7

```
       5    8   12
 1  2  6    9   13
    3  7   10   14
    4      11   15
```

add on, P 208-209
Florian Haydn: 1-5, 7-9, 14, 15
Peter Fattinger: 6, 10
Michael Nagl: 12
Michael Strasser: 11, 13

Creative Space Agency, P 212-213
Creative Space Agency

1	3 6
	4 7
	8
2	5 9

Zwischenpalastnutzung, P 216-217
Christoph Petras: 1
Markus Bader und Jan Liesegang,
Raumlabor Berlin mit Alexander
Römer: 2, 8
Florian Haydn: 3, 4, 6, 7
David Baltzer: 5, 9

| 1 | 3 |
| 2 | 4 |

einfach-mehrfach, P 220-221
Stadt Wien, MA 18 /
Mehrfachnutzung: 1
Kids Company: 2-4

Kioskisierung, P 224-225
Jens Fischer, Peter Arlt,
Benjamin Foerster-Baldenius

1	4	
2	5	7
3	6	

OpTrek, P 228-229
Sabrina Lindemann: 1-4, 6, 7
Jan Körbes: 5

	3	5 9
	4	6
1		7
2		8 10

Houthavens, P 232-233
EN Architecten, Stichting
Werkspoor: 1, 3-7, 9, 10
DRO Amsterdam: 2
D. F. Eberhardt: 8

bed by night, P 236-237
Han Slawik

Bibliographic information published by Die Deutsche Bibliothek

Die Deutsche Bibliothek lists this publication in the Deutsche National-
bibliographie; detailed bibliographic data is available in the internet
at http://dnb.ddb.de.

© 2006 Birkhäuser – Publishers for Architecture,
P.O. Box 133, CH-4010 Basel, Switzerland
Part of Springer Science+Business Media

This book is also available in a German language edition
ISBN-10: 3-7643-7459-4, ISBN-13: 978-3-7643-7459-4
Printed on acid-free paper produced from chlorine-free pulp. TCF ∞

Translation: David Skogley, Steven Lindberg
Layout: Richard Ferkl, Vienna
Typesetting: Jo Schmeiser, Vienna
Printing: Remaprint, Vienna

ISBN-10: 3-7643-7460-8
ISBN-13: 978-3-7643-7460-0

www.birkhauser.ch

9 8 7 6 5 4 3 2 1